CORNWALL'S FORGOTTEN CORNER

CAWSAND, KINGSAND, MILLBROOK, ST. JOHN
AND SHEVIOCK

by

Tony Carne

First published 1985

© TONY CARNE 1985

ISBN 0 946143 13 7

Printed by E. J. Rickard Ltd.,
11-13 Holborn Street, Plymouth, Devon.
Tel: 0752 660955

CONTENTS

TO UNCLE ROY

ACKNOWLEDGEMENTS

I am grateful to the following who have either given me information or have kindly loaned photographs for inclusion in this book.

Margaret Bartlett · Jim Broad · Roy Clift · Leah Crowley · Roy Carne · Roy Sullivan · Bill Dunstone · Crispin Gill · Rex & Ann King · Frank Kingwell · Eric Marks · Pat & Freda Manning · Mike Mashford · Henry Pryn · Rodney Snowden

A.C.

All modern photography by Pat & Freda Manning, Colyn Thomas.

PREFACE

At the extreme south eastern corner of Cornwall is Rame Head, a massive, brooding pile of slate which juts out into the sea dominating the coastline amidst steep cliffs and jagged rocks. The Rame Peninsula is the name which is loosely applied to the narrow strip of land which lies immediately behind the coast, washed on the northern flanks by the Lynher and Tamar Rivers, and on the east side by the waters of Plymouth Sound. It comprises the ancient parishes of Maker, Rame, Saint John and Sheviock.

This is Cornwall's Forgotten Corner. Forgotten in the historical sense, because part of it was once included in Devon. Forgotten in the modern sense because, thanks to its isolation, it escapes the tourist hordes as they grind their way over the Tamar Bridge to fight their way down country though the monoxide fumes to the caravan parks, the amusement arcades and the trashy gift shops. Cornwall's forgotten corner is uncommercialised; a haven for those who enjoy the leisure pursuits of the countryside, rambling, bird watching and sea angling. Thanks again to its relative inaccessibility it has, so far, largely escaped the ugly hand of the 20th century developer and retains much of its charm. How long it will remain unspoilt however, is open to question for there have been extensive modern developments at Torpoint, and other places, despite the restrictions imposed on residents by the Ferry and high local unemployment. Visitors who wish to avoid delays at Torpoint are recommended to use the Ferry bus service to Cawsand or Cremyll ferry. During the summer months there is also a ferry boat service to Cawsand beach from the Mayflower Steps in Plymouth.

The Rame Peninsula is 'Walkabout Country' in its truest sense and this book has been written principally for the rambler or resident, who wishes to learn something of the background to some spectacular scenery. Not surprisingly the area abounds with artists and photographers whose work is in much demand. Together with walking, the two other most popular countryside leisure pursuits are angling and bird watching, and I am indebted to boh Peter Carne and Bob Hannaford for providing the notes which are included in the appendices at the rear of this book.

A.C.
July 1985

PREFACE TO SECOND EDITION

Since writing 'Cornwall's Forgotten Corner' five years ago I have gained a great deal more information on the subject which has necessitated the rewriting of certain parts. There have also been changes. Changes which in common with many parts of Britain neither enhanced the countryside nor the quality of life of its inhabitants. Ironically it has happened at a time when, according to Steve Madge (Appendix III) local interest and concern for the countryside has never been greater. Neverthless much remains to interest and charm resident and visitor alike.

A.C.
April 1990

FOREWORD

Tony Carne has two essential attributes of the good local historian, a deep personal knowledge of his territory and the scholarly ability to research and evaluate its distant past. On top of that, his family has been living in Rame and the area for generations, if not centuries, and he has from an early age stored up the stories of those relatives and had the wisdom to write down their anecdotes and those they too remember being told by their fathers and uncles.

Before becoming a school teacher he travelled the world as a naval officer, so he has a wide outlook; he can see his own land in the light of other places, and what can happen to quiet corners when the world becomes too pressing.

I too have known this forgotten land; when I was a child the fishing families of Portwrinkle where I spent much time, the Dawes, the Pengellys and the Andrews, still fished in fine weather and cultivated their potato patches on the cliffs in winter, still used donkeys to bring up seaweed to fertilise those patches and in time the donkeys carried up the potatoes in panniers strung across their back. One family hardly spoke to another; for that matter they were a silent race, hardly speaking to each other. I am old enought to have known the buses, the rival boats, even wagonettes to Whitsands that Tony writes of.

In those days Cawsand was the expensive place. When we Plymothians went down to ''the Quay'' — nowadays everyone calls it the Barbican — for a day on the beach, Bovisand was 6d return and Cawsand 9d, so we always went to Bovisand. Times were hard. In those days Cawsand had more day trippers than it has now; and there were plenty of day-tripper boats coming into the beaches all through the summer and people then were willing to carry their picnics, and to walk. Now they must go by car, and Torpoint Ferry means delays, and the car parks are small, so Cawsand and Kingsand are far less used.

Even in Plymouth, just a couple of miles across the waters of the Sound, you will find very few people who know even Kingsand and Cawsand, or have been there once or twice in a lifetime. In England, by which I mean the other side of the Exe, you will hardly find a soul who has ever heard of the place.

Long may it continue. I do not wish Tony or his publisher anything but success with this splendid book, but its sale ought to be restricted to bona-fide lovers of this secret land. As it was said in another (and unprintable) context, this is too good for all but special people.

Crispin Gill

1. CREMYLL, MAKER AND MOUNT EDGCUMBE

Cremyll is the traditional gateway into the Rame Peninsula. Indeed, the Cremyll Ferry marks the start of one of the three routes of antiquity down into Cornwall. This route, the southernmost of the three, ran across the ridges and involved other ferry crossings at Looe, Bodinnick, Par and King Harry, on its way to Penzance. Cremyll owes its existence to the Ferry, and it is worth pausing to see how it has influenced the area.

The earliest records of the Ferry date from the 12th century, but it must have been established long before, possibly during the Bronze Age, (2,500 BC). By the early years of the 8th century the Saxons of Wessex had gradually pushed the Cornish from their lands in Devon back as far as the River Tamar. The Cornish did not take kindly to this and, allied with the Danes, frequently crossed the river to make raids into Saxon territory. The riverside settlements were collectively known as Tamarworth, and to secure them against these attacks, the Saxon kings annexed the part which was to become the parish of Maker. With the west bank of the river and the high ground overlooking the estuary in their possession, the Saxons effectively controlled the river. Maker thus became the first part of Cornwall to come uner English domination. In 825, Egbert, at Hingston Down, beat the combined Danish and Cornish armies, and a century later Athelstan subjugated the rest of Cornwall and fixed the Cornish border along the River Tamar. The anomaly of 'Maker in Devon' arises from the fact that that land had been given to the Bishop of Sherborne, who later transferred it to the king of Wessex, along with a parcel of land on the eastern shore of Plymouth Sound. Subsequent to this the land was always the possession of a Devon landlord, and became part of Devon. It remained so until an Act of Parliament of 1844.

The Tower House, Cremyll

Cremyll Ferry

It is evident then, that a ferry was essential to serve this outpost of the Saxon Kingdom. The name Cremyll itself is thought to be a Cornish word meaning crooked pool. A hill stands behind the boatyard, and forms part of a limestone bed which extends across the river to Mount Wise, Stonehouse, and the Hoe, to end at Oreston.

In medieval times the Ferry was of great importance, and it carried most of the Cornish mail up until 1791 when the new, rival ferry at Torpoint gained the contract. The 1760 turnpike road ran from here to Crafthole, on its way to Liskeard; the old Toll Cottage still stands at the side of the road by the car park.

The original crossing was from 'Cremell Point' — now part of the Victualling Yard — to Barn Pool. Strong tides run here and in the days before the Breakwater was completed, in 1840, the crossing could be hazardous. Several writers have commented upon having had hair-raising experiences in foul weather. The boat carried both traveller and horse. In 1764, the owner of the inn at Cremyll advertised a large boat with terms ranging from a coach and six 5s, to a single horse chaise 1s 6d The boat was manned by five oarsmen but, even when sail assisted, the crossing could take well over an hour. November 1701 saw a severe gale in which seven people were drowned, and during the disastrous winter of 1777 three boats were lost.

Cremyll's heyday undoubtedly came during the 18th century: the period which coincided with the building of the Naval Dockyard. Queues were frequent, and an additional boat to Mutton Cove was provided in 1741. Although the Edgcumbes, who owned both the ferry and the land on either side of the river, welcomed the increase in trade, they did not relish the extra traffic which now made its way up through the garden and past their house. In 1730 they moved the landing place from Barn Pool to Cremyll and extended their house and gardens. The present road which makes its way up the hill past the lodge dates from this time also.

The Edgcumbes were also troubled by competition from some free-lance Millbrook sailors operating from Foss, Ware and Empacombe and these infringements upon their monopoly were eventually settled by a series of lawsuits in 1777. Admirals Hard dates from 1824, when the Navy acquired the 'Cremell Point' landing, along with ten acres of adjoining land, for building the Royal William Yard. A further six acres were reclaimed from the sea. The quay at Cremyll, opposite the inn dates from 1836/37.

As the progressive Victorian age wore on the old ferry boats became outmoded. There was great dissatisfaction with timings and comfort, for example, in January 1877 it was claimed, with irony, that 'the special express ferry starting at one o'clock almost always succeeds in reaching Stonehouse Hard by half past two'. Such inefficiency could no longer be tolerated and in 1885 the pulling boats were superceded by a steamer, the Dodo which provided a much faster service with covered accommodation. An added improvement was that vehicles and horses towed astern in a barge. The fare for a carriage, or wagon was 3s 6d return, a cart, and later a car, cost 2s 6d A hearse cost 10s 6d, and if it contained an occupied coffin, one guinea. The barge or horseboat, as it was known, had to. be manhandled into position for disembarkation; no easy task. To facilitate matters on the Cremyll side, a handwinch was used which still stands outside the ferry turnstile. The horseboat service ceased in the 1930s when horse-drawn gave way to motorised vehicles which found it easier and quicker to go by way of Torpoint.

By the early years of the century there were three steamboats in service, the Carrier, the Armadillo and the Shuttlecock. The latter two were built in the nearby boatyard, which has always had strong connections with the Ferry, and at that time was run by the Waterman family. The boatyard occupies the site of a former limestone quarry, early nineteenth century documents refer to it as Franks' Quarry, and it is evident that vast quantities of rock have been evacuated. The remains of caves have been discovered, but we can only speculate upon what might have been there before quarrying commenced. By 1927 all of the old steamboats had either been wrecked or broken up and the boatyard, now run by Rogers, built Armadillo II and Shuttlecock II. In 1945 the Earl of Mount Edgcumbe sold the ferry service, plus boats, to the Millbrook Steamboat Company who re-named the boats Southern Belle and Northern Belle. The boatyard, now run by Mashford Bros., fitted them with diesel engines in the same year. The ferry service is now operated by Tamar Cruising who still retain the services of the old Shuttlecock II or Northern Belle.

During World War II two of the ferry crew were killed by a bomb whilst standing outside the Cremyll shelter. A bomb also demolished a Cremyll landmark, the Tower House which had stood near to the Boatyard entrance. The young Plympton painter Joshua Reynolds took a lively interest in the work here in the 1730s, when he was under the patronage of Richard Edgcumbe.

The Edgcumbe Arms, Cremyll

The inn at Cremyll, the Edgcumbe Arms, has not always been so named. In former times it had been variously known as the Passage House and the Ferry Inn. The present house was taken in 1762 by Ralph Banks, a former steward to Commodore Edgcumbe who advertised a 'large and very commodious inn with six good and well fitted lodging rooms.' In 1796 a discerning traveller declared it to be 'an excellent house with good beds and victuals of all sorts'. This bore a sharp contrast to the vast majority of Cornish inns which were notoriously grim in all respects. The inn needed to be comfortable, for in the pre-Breakwater days travellers were often stranded by rough weather which prevented the ferry from running.

The pub was kept busy around the turn of the century by the presence of three naval training ships. Invincible, Implacable and Impregnable, which were moored off Cremyll. A trainee's life aboard one of these hulks was spartan in the extreme. Decks were holystoned before breakfast, the rigging was climbed and swimming instruction proceeded regardless of the weather. All of it was accompanied by a constant babel of shouted orders which for decades was part of the Cremyll scene. On Sundays the trainees were allowed ashore with the pub as their first port of call. There was so much rowdyism that the licence was cut to six days, but the more resourceful members took to supping their ale from teacups which were frequently topped up from extra-large teapots.

When the hulks moved as a result of the 1920s Defence cuts, it was said that the Cremyll climate changed, so effectively had they sheltered the hamlet from the north east.

The land behind Cremyll to the south west is often missed, since the spectacular scenery of Mount Edgcumbe draws visitors in that direction. For the rambler wishing to explore this area there is a charming footpath which hugs the shoreline as far as Lower Anderton, from where the more energetic can climb the hill to Maker Church.

The footpath is signposted Empacombe, and starts immediately opposite the Toll Office. It passes some bungalows and what was once a Chapel of Ease and schoolroom. There is a former quarry on the left; the path rises and skirts the rear of the Boatyard, to rise and level off just below the Obelisk which sits atop the knoll. The Obelisk was erected circa 1770 by Timothy Brett, a former commissioner of the Navy, in memory of his friend George, 3rd Baron Edgcumbe.

Beneath the Obelisk are the remains of the 18th century Cremyll Redoubt and Musketry Lines, adjoining the old Admiralty Sports Field. Beyond them is an obsolete pumping station, a relic of World War II, intended to pump fuel oil to storage tanks further up the hill.

On the northern side the view across the water is completely different. The Hamoaze stretches away past the Dockyard and Torpoint, clear up to Bull Point. Here, in the largest dockyard in Europe, may be seen British warships as well as visitors from NATO and other foreign countries.

Immediately opposite the Obelisk is the oldest part of the Dockyard; almost 300 years old. There is the 'King Billy' figurehead, the oldest covered slipway in the world dating from the early 19th century, a dry dock, and the Great Slipway. The first ship to be built at Plymouth Dock, as Devonport was called until 1824, was the 73 ton, 4 gun *Postboy* of 1694. Other famous names which have been launced here include the 100 gun, 2164 ton *Royal Sovereign* of 1786; Beatty's *Jutland* flagship, the battlecruiser *Lion* of 1910 (26,000 tons) and the 1913 battleship *Warspite* (30,000 tons). Around the turn of the century Cawsand schoolchildren would be given a half holiday to assemble here to watch the launch of a big ship which their fathers had helped to build. I saw the frigate *Plymouth* launched here in 1959.

In contrast to the bustle of the harbour is the tranquillity of Empacombe, the empty coombe, with its picturesque little harbour cottages and gardens. John Rudyerd had his Eddystone lighthouse workyard here in 1706, and it was last used for servicing the old training hulks. Behind the high folly wall are gardens where the Mount Edgcumbe vegetables were once grown, and above them the Home Farm. Empacombe is overlooked by a disused windmill, which had replaced an earlier mill on the Maker Heights, and is one of only six left today out of

Ruins of Empacombe Windmill

sixty which were shown on Martyn's 1749 map of Cornwall. Alongside is a limestone quarry and a kiln, a reminder of the days when the main fertiliser used on the fields, apart from farmyard manure, beach sand and seaweed, was lime. The kilns were charged with limestone and coal and then fired. The whole process would last up to ten days. This particular kiln was the last one in the area to be used regularly, and was last fired in the early 1920s. The other kilns at Cawsand and Millbrook, fell into disuse long before this. To operate them the limestone had to be shipped out by barge from Cattedown, but at Empacombe the stone was already on site.

Empacombe Redoubt, to the west of the quarry is of the Napoleonic era and dates from 1812. The footpath keeps to the shoreline below the Redoubt, giving fine views of Millbrook Lake and across to Southdown. It crosses the road just before Lower Anderton and makes its way inland and upwards, past Nanny Parson's Grove and eventually reaches Maker Church.

The strip of land extending westwards from here along the southern shore of Millbrook Lake was part of 'Maker in Cornwall', and was part of the ancient Schyndelhall or Shilhall estate. The house is currently called Tudor Cottages, but it is far older than this name suggests. The whole area along the shore of the lake here comprises Lower Anderton, and the next group of houses are known as Wear (or Weir) Cottages. The weir would have been a fish weir, a long net, suspended on poles across the current, in which fish were caught on an ebbing tide.

Halfway up the hill overlooking Shillhall is another pumping station and oil storage tanks, which the footpath skirts before entering the wood. Where the path crosses the road it is worthwhile making a small detour of fifty yards down the hill to visit the holy well of Saint Julian. Julian was a medieval saint who was often associated with hostelries and ferry men. The well, is above the bank behind the horse trough, and is inside a medieval well house (restored in 1882). There had been a holy well here since the 6th century, when a Celtic missionary worked in the district, and as in most cases of this sort, the well was no doubt an earlier pagan shrine adopted for Christian use. The holy man may well have been Saint Sulyan of Luxulyan. At this time the Celtic peoples of Ireland, Wales, Brittany and Cornwall shared a common language and culture. The Celtic church had long been established in Ireland and it was from there that the missionaries went out and converted their Celtic brethren to Christianity. These saints are commemorated in place names all over Cornwall, Wales and Brittany.

Maker Church may well date from this era, and was almost certainly built upon the remains of some earlier structure. The Celts usually built churches close to Holy Wells, sometimes in relatively isolated places. The name of Maker itself offers another clue for the siting of the church. In Cornish, ''magor'' means ruin or old walls, and at Magor in West Cornwall there are ancient Roman remains. So, it is possible that the original church was built on the site of, and using the same materials as, a Roman stockade or watch tower which had been abandoned centuries before.

In about the year 1500 Maker Church was demolished, and much of the present building dates from Tudor times. There were extensive restorations during the last century; the Edgcumbe family influence is evident in a chapel where stained glass and monuments effectively chart the family's rise to fortune. The pillars of the Edgcumbe chapel supposedly came from an older chapel in Bere Ferrers. The church was restored in 1874 when the three decker pulpit and galleries were removed. The font is of moor stone and is similar to the fine Norman font at Bodmin. It was removed to Maker from the ruined church of Saint Constantine in Saint Merryn in 1840.

The tower is sixty five feet in height and is a conspicuous land and sea mark. The belfry contains six good bells. During the French wars of the 18th century the tower was used to communicate shipping movements to the Dockyard. In the 1779 invasion scare, during the American War of Independence, the signals indicated that an enemy fleet of eighty eight French and Spanish ships was in sight. Fortunately it came to nothing: a copy of the signal codes is exhibited in the church alongside the old parish stocks. Also exhibited is a copy of Reynold's portrait of Thomas Smart, vicar of Maker, painted from an original sketch made whilst Smart was preaching and drawn on the twelve year old artist's thumbnail. The monuments include one to the Rev Whiddon who collapsed and died whilst preaching in the church in 1866. There is a sundial mounted on the south porch dating from 1768, and inside is a holy water stoup now restored to its original position.

The graveyard contains much of interest, including the headstone of a child

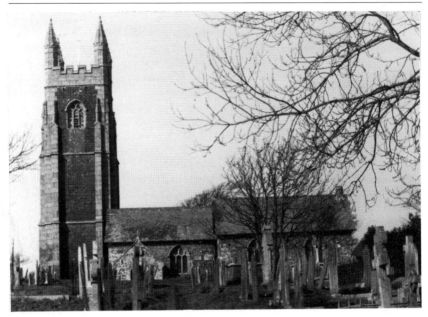

Maker Church

who died after swallowing a stone, the 1849 cholera pit, and the Edgcumbe family vaults. Among the traditions connected with Maker Church is that of the Lady Mount Edgcumbe who was interred when in a trance, and on being roused by the sexton trying to steal her ring, rose up, walked home, and survived many years. An episode of the old smuggling days relates how the Vicar, having taken the Rural Dean to the top of the tower, espied twenty three kegs lodged in the gutter between the church roofs. Naturally they looked the other way and it is said that next morning there was a keg at the vicarage door.

In front of the church is Maker Church Green and it was here that the Maker Green Games were held up until the early years of the 19th century: although they survived for several decades afterwards in Millbrook. Most Cornish parishes held an annual feast, usually to commemorate the dedication of the church but by the mid-18th century the feast had usually degenerated into a drunken rout. At Maker the feast, or Games, took place at Whitsuntide and was a major summer event, attracting crowds from all over East Cornwall as well as from Plymouth. They were catered for by stalls set up by local pubs and the scale of it all may be judged by the prizes awarded. In 1753 a fine buff waistcoat, trimmed with gold lace was to be wrestled for, a silver laced hat to be cudgelled for, and a holland shift to be run for by women. The 1785 three-day event was even more ambitious and aimed at attracting a hard drinking, heavy gambling, money-spending crowd. There was bull baiting with a silver collar worth one guinea for the champion dog, cudgelling for a £5 silver bowl and wrestling for a 'large elegant silver bowl worth six guineas. Similar prizes were awarded both on the second and third days.

The Edgcumbe Memorial

Sundial Maker Church

In years of intense poverty such as 1757, the Games were suspended but the only other interruption to the revels was due to the attentions of the Press Gang. The presence of such a large gathering of fit, able-bodied young men inevitably made the Games a prime target for any ship's captain desperate to make up his crew. A popular ballad of 1810 relates how the Navy would wait until late afternoon before making their move. They would land at Empacombe or Hooe Lake and use the woods for cover before seizing the luckless victims, who by this time, befuddled by drink and wearied by the exertions of the day, were an easy prey.

From Maker Church the rambler may either continue on to Kingsand or return to Cremyll. There are two routes to Kingsand. The first one is by the footpath to Maker Farm, starting at the stile in the hedge. It passes to the rear of the 1724 former Vicarage, which is now a hotel and restaurant. The other route enters by the Park, passes the church on the right hand side, and descends the hill to join the Coast Path by Hooe Lake Cottage.

After the exertions of the climb from Cremyll, returning to the ferry is a much more leisurely affair. Enter the Park by the Car Park to the left and instead of bearing right for Hooe Lake take the left hand fork.

The path then leads down hill via the Dry Walk and gives magnificent views of the Hamoaze, Plymouth and Dartmoor beyond, with Kit Hill and Bodmin Moor clearly visible on the Cornish side. It is sobering to recall that just a few years ago the CEGB was proposing to build a multi-megawatt power station at Insworke Point in the immediate foreground. A chimney, as high above sea level as Maker Church tower, was to have been built which would have discharged hundreds of tons of corrosive sulphur dioxide into the atmosphere daily. The effects of such a development hardly bear thinking about. Mercifully, bodies such as the Tamar Valley Protection Society, delayed things sufficiently for the Arabs, in 1973, to hoist the price of oil high enough to cause the plan to be shelved. Constant vigilance is required however, for the CEGB still own the land at Insworke, and periodically announce fresh schemes to 'test the water'.

Beneath the Dry Walk is an ancient tumulus and Barrow Park, the cricket pitch is adjacent to it. The path then joins a drive by the car park which leads to Mount Edgcumbe House, and finally sweeps down hill, past the pond and through the avenue to the Ferry.

The scene at Cremyll is dominated by Mount Edgcumbe House which is set in a prominent position overlooking the estuary in a landscape designed to enhance its beauty. The 865 acres which comprise the Country Park itself were purchased from the Edgcumbe family in 1970 by Cornwall County Council and Plymouth City Council. The Park is currently managed by a Joint Committee and, after years of neglect, is being restored.

Plans for building a house were made by Piers' son Richard in 1549, and four years later the fine Tudor mansion was completed. The Edgcumbe family seat then moved down from Cothele to Mount Edgcumbe, as the place was named, for it was then the fashion amongst the gentry to prefix the family name with Mount, as in Mount Wise Mount Gould etc.

Just one year afterwards, Richard entertained a group of foreign diplomats at the House, one of whom was the Spaniard Duke of Medina Sidonia who was destined to lead the Great Armada. Sidonia admired the house and, had the Armada been successful, it would have been his reward.

The Edgcumbes were always strong Royalists and when the Civil War came along they naturally supported the King. The House was garrisoned in 1643 and beseiged from May 1644 for one year before being surrendered to the Parliamentarians in 1646. The Restoration in 1660 saw the Edgcumbes' fortune return and in 1664 the House was extended. The extension was essential to support the Edgcumbes' social aspirations and the scale of the entertainment that was expected. The high living continued at Mount Edgcumbe up until the early years of this century when a scarcity of money caused by the Great War and Death Duties brought it all to a close.

Disaster struck the house in April 1941 when it was hit by a German incendiary bomb. The bomb fell into an attic where the Earl had been storing some of the possessions of Alnod Boger of Wolsdon. In 1939 Wolsdon had been requisitioned by the RAF as the Headquarters for the local Balloon Barrage and so storage space was required which the Earl gladly provided. Unfortunately his Lordship was very conscientious, and he insisted that the attic door be kept locked. This so hampered the firefighters that by the time they had opened the door the fire had gained a firm hold and the whole building was destroyed. The present structure resembles the original and was completed in 1962.

Behind the House were stables, coach house, workshops and a laundry. There was also a brewhouse. One of the brewers was Sam Sowden, a very popular man since he always insisted that the workers sampled the brew thoroughly before passing it fit for His Lordship's consumption.

Mount Edgcumbe House, 1910

Saint Julian's Well, Maker, with the old horsetrough

THE ENTRANCE, MT. EDGCUMBE PARK.

Blizzard Damage, Mount Edgcumbe Park March 1891

The Coade Stone

The Garden Battery

Photographs by courtesy of Colyn Thomas

The Gardens fall into two categories, Formal and Landscaped, and are the result of generations of interest and enthusiasm by the Edgcumbes. They are remarkable, not only for their intrinsic beauty, but also as an example of the development of the English Country Garden between the years 1700 and 1815. The Gardens have been open to the public for over 200 years now, although access in the early days was limited to one day per month. A sign outside the Park read 'No dogs or Midshipmen': hooligans are not a modern phenomenon.

The first gardens to be laid down were in the formal stylised patterns which had been in vogue since the early 1400s. This fashion was to change in 1649 in the cultural revolution which accompanied the Restoration of the Monarchy. It was then that the influence of certain artists and poets, notably Milton and Thomson, brought in the era of the Landscape Garden. It was the age of Capability Brown. One of the disadvantages with this style was that it required the planting of numerous trees which took a man's lifetime to reach maturity, so, towards the end of the 18th century, the fashion changed and the gardens became formal once again.

Apart from the immediate vicinity of the House little remains of the original formal gardens. The more recent ones, however, are perfectly preserved, and it is these which a visitor normally encounters first.

Access to the Formal Gardens is gained through the lodge arch which stands to the left of the main Park Gate opposite the Information Centre. The gardens lie behind a deer-proof wall and hedge, upon an area of land which until 1779, had been wooded. A threatened invasion by the French and Spanish however necessitated the felling of all the trees along the shoreline to deny cover to potential invaders whose anticipated target would have been the Dockyard. Felling the trees produced two results. First, Admiral George Edgcumbe was elevated to Viscount in recognition of his patriotism, and second, the need to redevelop the stricken area, or Wilderness, was created.

The Edgcumbes reacted positively. Here was the opportunity, not only to establish a Formal Garden but also to introduce some of the new varieties of plant which were beginning to arrive in England from overseas. Friends of the Edgcumbes, the Harcourts of Nuneham in Oxfordshire, had engaged William Mason, the eminent landscape designer, to build a garden for them which was greatly admired. Mason duly came to Mount Edgcumbe in 1783 and supervised the layout of the lawns, flowerbeds and shrubberies which became known as the English Garden.

On passing through the lodge arch the visitor sees the most recent of the Formal Gardens, the Italian Garden. This was laid out in 1807 to display orange trees which had been brought back from Constantinople in the 1750s. The trees were housed in the orangery which was a gift to Richard Edgcumbe by Thomas Pitt of Boconnoc, Lord Camelford. Each spring the trees, in their tubs, were brought out and positioned, and, after producing blossom and fruit were put away again in the autumn. The Orangery was bombed in 1941 and all the trees died of frost damage, but the building has been restored and is now used as a teashop. The

Italian style fountain dates from 1803 and was also a gift, from Lord Bessborough, the second Earl's godfather. On the stairway opposite the Orangery are statues of classical deities, Apollo, Bacchus and Venus, and are replicas of Roman originals

If you ascend the steps and keep to the left you will pass the Summer Garden, and beyond that enter the French Garden. This was the favourite spot of Sophia, the wife of the second Earl, who erected an urn to her memory when she died in 1806. The garden has low box hedges which surround a shell fountain, facing which is the Octagon Room, with its convex mirror and conservatories on either side.

Beyond the French Garden lies Mason's English Garden. Its informality is in complete contrast to the rigidly styled French and Italian Gardens. Paradoxically for an English Garden it contains many of the foreign plant species which were introduced in the 1780s. They include a Maidenhair, Japanese Cedar, Cork Oaks, Palms, Fruit Salad and Handkerchief trees. The scene is completed with flowing lawns and a Georgian Dower House.

Flanking the English Garden to the westward is a small Spring Garden, whilst to the east is a Fern Dell. This is a former quarry containing a spring, several archaeological and geological curiosities and a Pets' Cemetery. One of the pets wa a pig named Cupid, but unfortunately his headstone has been removed. King George III, on one of his visits to Mount Edgcumbe, was much amused when he saw the stone, and when Queen Charlotte enquired as to what was the source of his amusement, he chuckled ''It's the family vault, Charly, the family vault...''

The Dower House in the English Garden

The gardens are protected on the exposed seaward side by a great ilex hedge which is 300 feet long, over 31 feet high, and took two men a fortnight to trim. At the base of the ilex hedge on the shore side is a bowling green/tennis court with an ancient Blockhouse at the north end. This Blockhouse matches Henry VIII's fort on the opposite side of the river, and dates from the late 1500s.

The Blockhouse saw most of its action during the Civil War when its three small guns were used against boats going into Stonehouse; Plymouth was a Parliament stronghold. In May 1644 some 300 men attacked and captured it, presumably it was on this occasion that one of the gun ports was damaged by a cannon ball. The invaders then went on to attack the House and take Maker Church, used as a signal tower, a battery of three guns at Cawsand, then to capture Millbrook and another battery of six guns at Insworke Point. After this the raiders awaited high tide and withdrew to Plymouth on the ebb, with captured guns and cattle.

Between the Blockhouse and the French Garden is a curious looking monument, a Coade Stone. This was erected in 1791 by Admiral George Edgcumbe to the memory of the same Timothy Brett who had erected the Cremyll Obelisk. It stands on three sculptured tortoises and quite possibly was chosen from a catalogue as three similar monuments exist elsewhere. Coade Stone was manufactured by the Coades to a secret formula which became lost when the last member of the family, a widow, died in the 1790s.

The Orangery in the Italian Garden

The Summer House in the French Garden

Adjacent to the Blockhouse is the Garden Battery. It was built in 1863 on the site of an earlier saluting battery and mounted twenty one guns, of which only three remain. The originals were taken from a French frigate and bear the mark RF with the Cap of Liberty and a date in the Revolutionary Calendar. On the rocky shore next to the Battery are the remains of more recent conflicts, the foundations of an engine house from where the anti-submarine boom was controlled during two World Wars.

Overlooking the lawn to the north of the Blockhouse is the Doric pavilion known as Thomson's Seat. It was this scene, in the 1720s, which inspired the poet, James Thomson to write the poem, 'The Seasons'. The poet is better known for having written 'Rule Britannia', but it is a verse from his 'Seasons' whch is inscribed upon a wall plaque in the pavilion. Another prominent feature here is the Wellingtonia, a giant sequoia, or redwood tree. Seeds were brought from California in 1853 and were named after the Duke who had died a year previously.

The Landscaped Gardens are found by following the path through the wicket gate at the far end of the bowling green. The route is signposted 'Coast Path', and passes a site where an American Engineer Battalion was encamped in the months prior to D-Day. The Americans were not idle during their wait and constructed concrete roads in the park as well as making many similar improvements in the Rame area. The troops used amphibious vehicles and a special slipway was built for them at Barn Pool. Several centuries ago the settlement

The Fern Dell with Pets' cemetery

of West Stonehouse is believed to have existed near here. The village paid for its vulnerability by being sacked by the French in 1350, although as we have seen the Cremyll Ferry continued to land here up until 1730.

During springtime the wooded hillside opposite the Gardens is carpeted with a magnificent display of daffodils which the road skirts as it rises to the Dripping Stone and then gently falls away as it approaches the Duck Pond. The barn, to which the anchorage, Barn Pool, owes its name, now exists only on old maps, where it is shown to the northern side of the pond. In George Edgcumbe's day the fleet would anchor here and Admiral Keppel was a frequent visitor to the House. It was also here, in the deeper waters of the estuary, that the storm-stricken brigantine 'Catharina von Flensburg' foundered in December 1786. Almost two hundred years were to pass before her cargo of reindeer hides and hemp saw the light of day again.

The Informal Gardens effectively commence here with a short U-shaped valley; since 1808 known as 'The Amphitheatre'. The Edgcumbes were quick to realise its potential, and designed a free and natural landscaped garden. Tiers of trees and a stream with miniature waterfalls and pools, lead down to the pond. Later, flower beds were planted, hydrangeas predominating in summer; whilst in spring the rich camellia and rhododendron blooms provide a touch of luxury.

To set off this classical scene was added the Temple of Milton, an Ionic rotunda situated by the shore. Inscribed inside is an extract from Paradise Lost in which the poet describes the Garden of Eden.

> *.. Overhead up grow Insuperable height of loftiest shade,*
> *Cedar and fir, and pine and branching palm,*
> *And sylvan scene and as the ranks ascend*
> *Shade upon shade. A woody theatre*
> *Of stateliest view.*

How entirely appropriate are these lines, and how clearly can the poet's inspiration be felt in the design of this landscape.

From the Amphitheatre the path climbs upwards to the Folly. This is an artificial ruin, for just as temples were an essential part of a classical landscape, so too were ruins of deep romantic significance. If no genuine ruin existed then you built one, as Richard Edgcumbe did in 1747. This particular ruin or folly, however deserves a closer look, some of the finely dressed pieces of granite are far too good for use in a mere ruin; or for the obelisk either, which had formerly occupied the site. These stones are believed to be all that now remains of the Chapel of St. Lawrence which had once stood near where the Royal William Yard gate now stands. Other fragments have also been used in the Gothic Seat above Picklecombe.

The Doric Pavilion — Thomson's Seat

The Temple of Milton

The Coast Path dips here and passes down through the Beechwood. Before turning upwards again it passes Lady Emma's Cottage which was built in 1876 to replace an earlier one destroyed by fire. A gardener who lived here with his young family in 1891 told the story of the ninth of March when the Great Blizzard struck the South West. Beechwood bore the brunt of the storm and they spent the night in a state of terror and suspense as the gale howled around the cottage and the great trees crashed down all around them. Miraculously both house and family were spared but daybreak saw a scene of devastation, four hundred beeches lay on the hillside amid shattered stumps and tangled roots in what was the greatest disaster the Park had experienced. Similar damage occurred during the storms of January 1990.

Above the Beechwood and the Folly, the Great Terrace runs from the House around to Picklecombe. The two mile long carriage drive follows the contour line, winding around the hillside above the cliff, giving alternate views of coastline and countryside. Started by the first Baron in the early 1700s, his successors extended it, first to Kingsand, then to Penlee Point. If we include the bridle path to Rame Head, we have six miles of rich and varied scenery to rival anything in the British Isles, with each turn of the way offering a fresh vista or curiosity.

Just such a vista is that which is to be enjoyed from above the Folly, with a panorama of The Hamoaze, Plymouth, St Nicholas (Drake's) Island, The Sound and the Dartmoor Hills in the background. Curiosities abound also, for just a short step beyond we have the fine arch which sits astride the Terrace above

Redding Point. Before 1770 this arch housed the High Street gate of the town of Stonehouse, much of which was Edgcumbe property. Rendered obsolete by 18th century traffic, it was transported here, where it formed a decorative part of a deer proof barrier around what had once been the Park's outstanding gem, the Zig-Zag Gardens. A sheltered nook, where exotic species flourished, in 1756 they formed a series of zig-zagging paths, from the Red Seat on the hilltop down to the seashore beneath. The lower zig-zags have fallen into the sea long since but enough remains of the Summer House with its camellias, palms, mimosa and myrtle to be able to imagine the scene which had charmed King George and Queen Charlotte during their visit of 1789. It was shortly after this that the Viscount was created Earl of Mount Edgcumbe.

Beyond the Zig-Zags the Terrace winds around Picklecombe Valley, which was once overlooked by the Gothic Chapel Seat. It must be remembered that when the gardens were in their prime the view over the Sound was virtually unobscured by the trees which have grown to maturity since. The walk is so sheltered and enclosed here that it almost comes as a surprise when we get a glimpse of the sea. So much greater then is the impact made by the Breakwater, seen framed between the trees. From the Southern Terrace it is just one mile distant and prior

The Folly, Mount Edgcumbe

Cremyll Ferry, Horsebus and Hulks

Cremyll with HMS Impregnable

The Italian Garden

Mount Edgcumbe House after the bombing

Photographs by courtesy of Colyn Thomas

to its construction Plymouth shipping had suffered such damage during south and south easterly storms that Earl St Vincent recommended that 'an artificial reef be constructed'. It was an ambitious project but in 1811 the Admiralty approved John Rennie's plans for a Breakwater. Rennie was later destined to build the Royal William Yard, but in 1812 work commenced at Oreston with the purchase of quarries and the building of railways. Two ton blocks of limestone were ferried out by specially constructed 'promiscuous barges' which dumped them in position. By March 1813 it had broken surface, and by 1815 a quarter of a mile was visible at low tide. But nature intervened in the form of violent storms, and instead of the estimated six years it actually took thirty years to complete. The lighthouse stone came from Luxulyan, the first stone of which was laid in February 1841 and the lantern first lit on June 1st 1844. The Breakwater was one mile long and had cost one and a half million pounds but 'it raised Plymouth from a moderate West of England town to a city of maritime eminence'.

Picklecombe Fort, now converted into private dwellings, dates from 1863 and was built upon the site of two former batteries of 1586 and 1848. When eventually completed in 1871, it linked with Bovisand and the Breakwater Fort to control the seaward approaches to Plymouth. Two tiers of 21 guns each (9 and 10 inch) were mounted, and then sealed in with massive armourplate. The guns, of 18 tons each, were removed in the 1920s; the army moved out in 1956. During the First World War an anti-submarine boom was used between Picklecombe and the Breakwater to close the harbour at night. Building of the Breakwater Fort began in 1868 and, after being used as a naval gunnery target, in 1887 fourteen twelve inch guns were fitted. It was all in vain however, for the forts were rendered obsolescent even as they were being built by the rapid development of gunnery technology, and they remain as monumental follies to shortsighted military planning.

The terrace around Picklecombe leads to a wild area known as the Earthquake, where the old cork trees are still growing. The original carriage drive now twists back around Hooe Lake valley, up to Maker Church and then back to the House. The curious name Hooe is a mispelling of Hoe, as in Plymouth Hoe, where it refers to a point of comparatively high land overlooking Plymouth Harbour. A lake in Cornwall can be anything from a pool or a stream to a river, so in Hooe Lake, we have a stream and a ridge.

At Hooe Lake is the Huntsman's Cottage and a navigation beacon. At the base of the short cliff is a series of dolerite dykes which are of interest to geologists. Grotton Plantation sits on the crown of the hill, where there are the remains of various Seats and a deer house. By Hooe Lake the Picklecombe Fort road crosses the Coast Path and follows a stream up to Maker Farm. This quiet, steepsided, wooded valley is a favourite haunt of the deer, and it is very pleasant to stroll from Kingsand to Hooe Lake and then return by way of Maker Farm and Heights. The farm occupies the classic position for an old Cornish settlement, tucked away in a valley by a spring, and it is possible that the ancient Macretone was situated here. The fields above have yielded mesolithic flints and Domesday Book recorded 6 villagers, 8 smallholders and 4 slaves here with 60 acres of pasture. There are also more recent historic remnants in the shape of fortifications which over the last three centuries turned Maker into one huge fort and reflect the increased importance of Plymouth and the need to protect it. The church clerk of the 1790s summed it up with

> Maker is a pretty place
> It looketh on Hamoaze
> And on it are some batteries
> To guard us from our foes.

Two early 20th century examples, Hawkins and Raleigh Batteries lie immediately south of the farm whilst to the north is No 5 Redoubt, a fine moated fort, on the far side of the road overlooking Millbrook Lake. The other four redoubts command Maker Heights and lie on a south west facing line across the isthmus. The first three are earthworks in the vicinity of the old barracks. Now overgrown, they were presumably used as rallying points for horse artillery. The fourth, another moated fort was later named as Grenville Battery; all five redoubts date from 1783-4.

The road leading to Kingsand passes Maker Farm and the entrances to Hawkins and Raleigh Batteries, to emerge in the open country of Maker Heights, presenting a spectacular view. The whole of Cawsand Bay and most of the Sound are framed by the Mewstone, Wembury and Bovisand to the east, with Mount Edgcumbe and the thickly wooded slopes of Penlee to the south and west. the open sea, and eventually France lies to the south-east. In summer the scene is particularly busy with dozens of small craft, both sailing and powered, scurrying around the Bay or rocking gently at anchor off Cawsand. A few fishing boats and larger vessels, such as the Brittany Ferries and the occasional warship heading for Plymouth, complete the picture, which sadly is not nearly as busy as in times gone by.

At night the scene can be magical. The navigation beacons faithfully winking out their warnings, and the brighter flash of the Breakwater Lighthouse contrasting with the silvery reflection of the moonlight on the water, give the place an air of enchantment. A moving green light shows where a ship is putting out to sea, the thump of diesel engines carrying clearly across the water: strange that the sound is not noticeable by day. And in the distance beyond the shadowy outline of Rame Head, the periodic double flash of the Eddystone indicates the main shipping lanes where giant tankers loom on the horizon, heading up Channel to their anchorage in Torbay.

Where the path forks there once was a military hospital. The well still exists, and the track beside it runs down a very pretty walk overlooking the Bay to Kingsand by way of Devonport Hill. In the days of long overseas commissions the naval wives of the village took this route in to Devonport Dockyard to collect their monthly allotments; hence the name Devonport Hill. Maker Barracks stands away to the right on the high land. It was built in 1769 and inspected by George III in the same year. The old Barracks and the Nissen huts, which were erected during the last war were last used as a schools' summer camp. During the last

Panoramic View of Kingsand and Sound circa 1800

war there were barrage balloons, anti-aircraft guns and rocket launchers situated
here. There is evidence of more ancient occupation also, for stone age flint
knappings have been found. The flints were certainly not mined at Maker, but
possibly were shaped here after being imported from Beer in Devon.

Grenville Battery lies just below the site of the Military Hospital. More recent
fortifications still futher down the hill from Grenville date from the 1870s and
are well preserved. At this point the road drops steeply away past some allotments
to Kingsand via a lane called Andiditch, possibly named after a Saxon earthwork.

Let us now return to Hooe Lake and continue our walk along the Coast Path
to Kingsand. The way climbs gently upwards to a grove of evergreen oaks, in
which is an old quarry from which a large amount of red building stone has been
taken. There are the remains of a fairly large track leading down to the beach
here, but it has long since become unusable. On emerging from the grove the
path dips downhill towards a small stream. In summer evenings the edges of the
track are festooned with glow-worms. Care should be taken when venturing off
the path, for adders are common here also. The beach below used to be known
as Warn Sandway; now it is simply Sandways. The bedrock changes abruptly
here, from the reddish slate and sandstone to pink volcanic felsite. To the west,
from Sandways Point, the shoreline resembles a lava flow which ends at Kingsand
beach.

At Sandways are items of industrial achaeology which have played a significant
role in the history of this area. The first building of interest is the old bark house,
now used as a summer dwelling, on the eastern side of the beach, beside a spring.
Fishermen would boil their nets and sails with oak bark to help preserve them.
The wedge-shaped structure is not connected with the fishing industry; it was
erected in 1875 to enable big guns to be landed and winched up the hill to Grenville
Battery overlooking the beach.

Sandways Point was the scene of a lively incident which occurred about a hundred years ago. All heavy goods coming to Cawsand came by sea, including vegetables from Devonport Market which were brought in by 'Market Boat'. This was a broad 20-footer and was usually crewed by Bill Jago and Sampy Oliver. Naval wives would sometimes cadge rides in the Dockyard to collect their allotments, although the most important cargo was beer for the village pubs. The beer was collected from Simmond's Tamar Brewery, where the hospitality was legendary. On this particular occasion Jago and Oliver had partaken much too freely, for it had seriously impared their judgment. As they engaged in pleasant banter with the women, who were perched high on the barrels, they cut too fine a line off the Point, and as the tide was ebbing the boat grounded; women, barrels and vegetables were all capsized into the water. Fortunately the commotion was witnessed by some observant fishermen on Kingsand beach, and they were quickly rescued, 'Skritchin and hollerin, buoyed up by their bloomers an bobbing around like corks'. Despite the happy outcome, the women never travelled in the Market Boat again.

The large building at the Kingsand end of the beach is one of the ancient Fish Cellars. Most of these were built in Elizabethan times for curing pilchards which were then abundant around the coast. The Cellars were probably the first large buildings to be erected near the village, and possibly their size gave rise to their being known as 'Palaces' (cf. Cornish Plas, court or seat).Elizabeth I decreed that there should be three meatless days in each week. One effect of this was to stimulate the fishing industry, and thereby create a sizable reserve of seamen. To satisfy the demand for fish, a pilchard curing industry quickly became centred upon Plymouth, it flourished and expanded, exporting fish to Roman Catholic countries on the continent and to Ireland.

Sutton Pool was becoming very congested by this time, and to avoid the taxes levied upon them by the Plymouth Corporation, the fish merchants decided to shift their operations. They came to Cawsand in about 1570, and considerably added the the already established fish-curing activities. At the high tide mark of the industry there were as many as ten cellars in operation, extending from Sandways right around the coastline to Sharrow Point in Whitsand Bay. The Cellars were first manned by seasonal workers, and teemed with activity. As the industry became more firmly established so also did the workers, who brought their families along with them and settled in the area. Most of the merchants rented the Cellars, but some prospered and settled also, the Trevilles of Rame Barton being one example; the names of others appear on the Benefactors' Boards in both parish churches.

The fish were netted in seines and brought ashore in maunds (large baskets) to the cellars, where women and children would 'bulk' them in alternate layers of pilchards and salt. "Train" oil for lighting was obtained by further pressing in hogsheads. The stench was overpowering, at St. Ives the vicar claimed that the smell was strong enough to stop the church clock. Most of the cellars have tiny harbours adjacent, often cut from the rock, where vessels could come alongside and embark their cargoes. The next Cellar along from Sandways, Cavehole Cellar, has a fine example of such a harbour, whilst still further along at Martin's Cove a considerable excavation has taken place, possibly for landing fish from nets. Between these two cellars is Longpool, which, although not connected with fishing, has served generations of Kingsand children as a paddling pool and a boating lake.

The Coast Path follows the Earl's carriage drive through the fields, known as Minadew, above the shore to Kingsand. Minadew in Cornish means black hillside and the hill above curiously enough is called Blackendown. As we have seen, the village was founded upon the fishing industry but exactly how the village became so named is open to speculation.

2. KINGSAND

The first recorded use of the name Kingsand appears in Edgcumbe family property transactions of the 1550s. Carew, writing in 1602, claims that the King in Kingsand was Henry VII. Carew visited the village in about 1580, and was told that at the end of the Wars of the Roses, in about 1484 Henry, then Earl of Richmond, sought to overthrow Richard III, and was supported by Richard Edgcumbe. Whilst cruising off the coast and conferring with his supporters, Henry anchored in Cawsand Bay and came ashore secretly for refreshment and to confer with Edgcumbe. When the King's men learned of Henry's whereabouts they set out from Plymouth to seize him, but Henry was warned and fled to his ship and thence back to France.

After the Battle of Bosworth in 1485 Henry became king. Richard Edgcumbe was knighted on the field of battle. The inn which he visited became known as the King's Arms; the lane, which led to the beach through the fish cellar, was called the King's Way, and the beach, King's sand.

Inn names, like fashions, sometimes change, and for a period this one was known as the 'Cawsand Volunteer', but in 1784 when Thomas Gray added a large extension, it was renamed the King's Arms. In 1910 the pub closed but the house is still called Kingsway House and the lane immediately opposite which converges with the Coast Path is the Kingsway. The fish cellar has now been redeveloped as a dwelling and public access to the beach is no longer available. It is an interesting tale; doubtless it was seized upon with relish by the local inhabitants of Kingsand in their age-old rivalry with the people who lived at Cawsand, or Cow's Sand.

Kingsand Beach about 1900

The twin villages of Kingsand and Cawsand run virtually on a north-south axis, clinging to the cliff side below Maker Heights, the Hats and Folly Hill. The two original settlements were probably in the areas of Fore Street/Market Street in Kingsand, and the Square at Cawsand. These developed in a linear coastal fashion until they became one. The steepness of the cliff face has resulted in a natural huddling of houses along narrow and tortuous thoroughfares, in many places too narrow to allow the flow of motor traffic. The buildings generally face the sea in a complex of shapes and colours in a charming irregularity and remarkable blend of building styles through the ages.

It would not be untrue to say that the villages owe much to the Royal Navy for their establishment and early development. The site beside the bay had all of the requirements for a human settlement bar one, security. It was with good reason that the ancients had clung to the heights of Maker and Rame, they were safe up there. Safe from the hordes of sea-borne raiders who infested the seas before the Navy gained its ascendancy during the 18th century. We have seen how West Stonehouse was destroyed, and as late as 1403 part of Plymouth itself was burnt by a Breton force. The vulnerability of coastal positions caused ports to be sited upriver where local pilots were needed to navigate and a castle would offer protection. Thus we have Saltash, the mother port on the Tamar, with Trematon Castle, Totnes on the Dart and Lostwithiel on the Fowey. As late as the 1770s Cornish fishermen dared not venture too far offshore for fear of being abducted by North African pirates and sold into slavery. These arabs were collectively referred to as 'Turks' and it is interesting to speculate as to how Cawsand came by its nickname of 'Turktown'.

Spiller's larker and seine boat off Martin's Cove.

Carew states in his Survey that Cawsand Bay was a refuge of the most noxious kind of seafarer who found shelter and fresh water there. Given these conditions it is unlikely that much existed here in medieval times other than a few fishermens' hovels. In time of war things were much worse, privateers, as well as pirates, frequently ransacked coastal towns and in an age when ships depended upon sail and tide, relief was difficult. Cawsand was a convenient place from which to attack Plymouth and for this reason Sir Richard Grenville installed a battery here in 1580 which beat off a Spanish attack in 1597. During the Civil War the Royalists denied the Bay to the Parliamentarian navy by building a stockade at Pemberknowse.

'Charlie' Chapman the painter in Fore Street, 1920.

Kingsand

Kingsand, Winter storm — Richard Marlow

The wars continued, against the Dutch, French and Spanish again, and it was possibly at the beginning of the 18th century that the Garrets were built. These are the defensive crenellations along Garrett Street; similar structures existed at Millbrook until a road improvement scheme swept them away in the mid 1980s. Other defences included the Amherst Battery in Heavitree Road and the Cawsand Bulwark which was sited up by the War Memorial.

It was during the late 18th century that the period of great architectural development occured which coincided with the period when Cawsand Bay was the principal anchorage of the Channel Fleet. The Channel Fleet spent most of its time blockading the French navy at Brest. When a strong south westerly sprang up the ships would repair to the most convenient shelter, Cawsand. The Navy brought security, and prosperity born of trade and the shadowy dealings of the smugglers.

Prosperity is reflected in the architecture; precious few Cornish fishing villages boast so many three storey dwellings. Extensions were made so that many of the buildings are externally deceiving due to alterations made over the centuries. In some, the older inner cores are still there and one has only to enter to see an interior from another age. Regrettably the modern 'open-plan' craze has resulted in the wholesale destruction of many fine interiors. On a similar note the character of the entire village is being ruined by an encirclement of tasteless and obtrusive examples of 20th century architectural mediocrity.

The older houses of the village are arranged around central, shared courtyards with restricted access. The houses were stepped back into the hill-sides and were built of the quarried rock. The court-yard clusters were not merely planned for social reasons; they provided privacy and, in less law-abiding times, security from intruders. The narrow entrance could easily be closed, and when necessary defence mounted against marauding sailors.

The Press Gang and Excise men also found that this narrow maze of unlit passages was not the easiest of places to hunt someone. Most of these old courts have now disappeared and have been re-developed, but a few remain both in Kingsand and Cawsand; their disappearance partially accounting for the seemingly haphazard house numbers. Higher and Lower Row are to some extent examples, originally there were no doors or windows of the ground floors facing the Green, neither was there a road in front. The road was made into the 1880s when the Earl of Mount Edgcumbe, wishing to gain easier access to his pheasants in Penlee Wood, made the New Cut, as it was called, to link up with New Road and avoid the congestion of Fore Street.

The grassy part of the Green is the site of a group of houses which were destroyed after being bombed in 1941. The larger houses bordering the Green date from a time when professional people began to make their homes in the village. Some of the fish merchants also lived here. Much of the financing for these large houses probably also came from smuggling, which inevitably was always closely associated with fishing and was widespread during the second half of the 18th century. Many show interesting external features and have pavements of white sea-shore cobbles in front of them. 'Algoma', although apparently an 18th century building was built around a much earlier core.

The Rising Sun Inn dates from this period. The publicans were frequently involved with fishing; many of them owned seine nets which were stored in lofts in the pub. After the catch had been sold the money would be shared out in the tap room, where much of it remained. The Mission Room, on the lower side of the lane from the Rising Sun, was given to the parishoners of Maker by the Edgcumbe family in 1876 for use as a meeting place. The local policeman the grocer were next, whilst further down still is the old Wesleyan Chapel, now converted into dwellings. At the bottom of the Green are some of the oldest houses in the village, lining narrow streets, which could accommodate nothing larger than a donkey cart. Some of the massive, hipped Cornish chimneys here suggest that the houses were built in the early 17th century.

Market Square, the area where Little Lane, the Green, Market Street and Heavitree Road all meet, is where the fishermen and farmers used to park their carts and barrows and sell their produce. A monthly cattle market was once held in the area between Little Lane and Market Street where Pebble House now stands. Before 1910 Heavitree Road was known as Back Street. It was close to the Wesleyan Chapel, and many of the Wesleyans, strict tee-totallers who never ventured inside a pub, lived there. On alternate Wednesdays however, the Exeter-based Heavitree Brewery provided a delivery service with a horse-drawn dray, and a good proportion of their trade was seen to be with the tee-totallers of Back Street. The fishermen, with characteristic humour, nicknamed the street Heavitree Road; a name which persisted and was eventually preferred to the less fashionable Back Street.

Halfway down Heavitree Road on the seaward side, the platform of the Amherst Battery is now the gardens of the Grey House, which itself stands on the powder magazine. Now much depleted and built upon, the Battery mounted twelve 18-pound cannon in 1770 when it was built during the French wars. Lord Amherst was the Port Admiral of the time, and the Battery, in conjunction with the Cawsand Bulwark, was intended to cover approaches to the beaches. It was considered inadequate and so the Maker Redoubts were constructed.

Fore Street was part of the principal thoroughfare through the village until New Road was opened to the public in 1920. Many of the older houses here are over two hundred years old, and have irregularly shaped door and window lintels. Here we have further evidence of how building materials were frequently salvaged and used again, for many of these old lintels are of solid oak and once formed the ribs and frames of old sailing vessels which were either wrecked or broken up on the village beaches. Local builders will tell how the floor joists of many of these old houses have similar origins.

Some of the windows still retain their square green tinged window panes. A few have a circular 'dew-drop' in the pane which shows that it was spun in a circular sheet from the central blob, and not laid down in a sheet as is the practice nowadays. It is said that a dew-drop window marked the home of a pensioner who was exempt from paying taxes; possibly the Window Tax, which was first levied by William of Orange, and which persisted until the 19th century. It was an early form of Income Tax, the wealthier a person was, the larger was his house and the more windows he had to pay tax on. The tax, of two shillings per window,

Kingsand, the old Institute

was avoided by simply bricking up the windows, and there are many of these blank windows still to be seen in the village. Most probably date from 1783 when the Tax was raised to compensate for the reduction in tea duty from 127% to 12½%. This was an early attempt to stamp out the smuggling of tea.

Maker Vicarage is at the upper end of Fore Street. The old Vicarage at Maker was too remote and expensive to maintain so the Vicar moved to Fore Street in the 1950s. The house was built for the Gray family in 1812 and reflects the general growth which the village experienced during the Napoelonic Wars. Doctor Gray was one of the last victims of the cholera epidemic of 1849; two of his daughters lived in the house until the first World War. At the top of Fore street is an old quarry, called Victoria Park. Opposite is the Community Hall, formerly St. Paul's Church with the Youth Club next door.

Just outside the village, opposite Coombe Park Council estate, is Watergate quarry where the local Scout organisation has its headquarters. Old maps show a building here with the name Elwell and the name lingers on at the nearby allotments at Andiditch, or Elwell Orchard. Large quantities of pink volcanic felsite have been taken from here both for building and roadstone, for which it had excellent qualities as it did not polish and so enabled horses to get a good grip. The local Council worked the quarry during the depression years of the 1920s with unemployed men breaking stones for the roads and when a road surface gets badly worn it is still possible in places to see the pink stones underneath. Before the advent of tarmac, roads were 'water-bound'. The stones were laid,

"Daddy" Spiller, an old Kingsand fisherman

earth was shovelled on, sprayed with water and then the whole lot was rolled in. In winter they soon became quagmires. The village streets were ankle-deep in mud, everyone had to wear boots, and many houses had mud-scrapers outside their front doors. The situation in Millbrook was so bad that a horse-drawn mud scraper had to be used to clear the streets. Motor vehicles made the problem worse. Their driving wheels would dig in to axle depth in winter, whilst in summer the rubber tyres lifted great clouds of dust. Tarmac solved these problems, but made life much harder for the horses, whose hooves could no longer dig into the road surfaces.

At the top of the hill beyond the quarry and Coombe Farm is Fourlanesend school, built in 1912 for boys of both Cawsand and Millbrook. It is now a Primary

School. The original school here was established by the church, with government assistance, in about 1840 and was known as Maker National School, later Free School. It was housed in the farm workers' cottages at the top of Millbrook road, next to the remains of the old animal pound. In the 1849 cholera epidemic the school was used as a hospital. My grandfather's uncle, John Carne, taught here for a while, and by all accounts was a 'bloody old tyrant'. He was so cruel that grandfather's brother Albert refused to go to school, and always blamed his uncle for his not becoming a scholar. John Carne later became a school inspector, and his advice to young teachers was terse, "Mark the boys, not the books". In 1832 he had been appointed Parish Relieving Officer. The Maker Workhouse was in Millbrook but in latter years destitutes were sent to Torpoint. In 1914 Fourlanesend was requisitioned as a military hospital, and the boys were dispersed to six different locations in Cawsand and Millbrook.

The lane behind the farm cottages leads to Treninnow farm, Wiggle and Whitsand Bay. It is not one of the original 'four lanes', because until 1850 it ended at Sollake farm, now derelict except for a barn. Sollake lies immediately below the school on the Millbrook road and has the only fields in the area where cattle may graze all year round. The lanes ending at this place led to Millbrook, Cremyll, Maker Heights and Cawsand. they have been considerably widened in recent years. Once they were lined with great elm trees with insufficient room for two carts to pass without one backing into a gateway.

Many of Kingsand's shops are in Fore Street. They include a newsagent/grocery, two quality gift shops and at the bottom, 'Shipshape' a general store specialising in up-market clothing and also housing the Post Office. Shipshape was formerly a grocery which in the early 1900s was lit by acetylene generated on the premises from calcium carbide. 'Top Drawer Gallery' halfway up the street, had been John Whittle's cobbler's shop back in the 1850s; he supplemented his business by selling second hand clothes from a donkey cart. It was not uncommon in those days for a tradesman to advertise his presence by a rhyme. On the signboard outside Whittle's the rhyme read

Stop stop stop, at the same old shop!
Here's a man that won't refuse
To sell you brand new boots and shoes,
And if the sole and heels are gone
He won't refuse to put new ones on.

It caught on immediately with the local boys who would shout the first line through the doorway and run away down Little Lane. There was no shortage of boys, or customers in those days either, in 1841 there were 42 people living in six houses in Little Lane.

One of Kingsand's most colourful characters, Granny Grills the smuggler lived in Gull Cottage which also houses 'Cottage Things'. Her maiden name was Susan Stone and she was born at Chivelstone in the South Hams of Devon in 1822. She was my grandmother's aunt and married Richard Grills, a fisherman, when she was 41. Ironically, her father had been in the Coastguard Service, and the family had moved from Prawle, with all their goods and chattels, by boat some years earlier. My grandmother used to recall how, as a small child in the 1870s, she would be taken by her aunt Susan across from Cremyll to Mutton Cove to deliver a skin of brandy to a Devonport pub. The skin would be dressed to look like a baby, and my grandmother, who was petrified by these excursions, was taken along to make the ruse more convincing. In the 1870s the smuggling in Cawsand had all but been surpressed, and was conducted on a very small scale compared to what had gone on previously. Fishermen, such as Richard Grills, would purchase the odd keg from French fishermen, and would land it concealed with their catch. The Mutton Cove route was preferred, because at that time it was only operated by watermen in pulling boats and was seldom watched by the Excise men. There had been trouble in 1825 with Cawsand women, smuggling brandy in bladders hidden under their skirts, bribing the Stonehouse watermen with 2d. to take them to Mutton Cove. This had caused a rumpus which had eventually involved the Earl and resulted in the ferry fairs being raised.

The photograph of Granny Grills shows what a formidable looking lady she was. On one occasion when an Excise man had commented on how quiet her 'baby' was, she retorted 'Yes me 'ansum, but there's plenty of spirit in 'un'. In later years she became blind, and lived with her sister Annie who was a staunch Wesleyan. One of my father's tasks as a boy was to go and read the bible to them; I still have that bible.

Granny Grills

When the cholera hit the village in the summer of 1849 there were 93 victims from Kingsand, most of whom lived in Fore Street and probably caught the disease from drinking sewage-contaminated water from the stream that runs behind the houses. Two of my grandfather's cousins were amongst the 116 who were buried at Maker. Their graves are marked with the letter 'C' inscribed on the reverse side of the headstone. There were 30 deaths in Millbrook and 21 in Cawsand.

The section of Market Street which adjoins the shore was formerly known as the Strand, and continued along what is now known as the Cleave. A cleave is a large cleft in a rock or shore; exactly where this particular cleave was is difficult to judge, for it has long been filled in and the road built over it.

In summer the Cleave is thronged with scores of holdiaymakers who enjoy the beach and the facilities provided by the Boatel, the Devonport Inn and a plastic fronted chip shop/amusement arcade. The scene of a hundred years ago was equally busy but instead of the leisure industry predominating, in those days it was fishing. The chip shop was a boatyard and the beach swarmed with fishermen repairing nets, crab pots and tending to their boats. Two centuries ago the Cleave Beach had extended further out to sea but the combined effects of the Breakwater diverting tidal currents and builders helping themselves have removed countless tons of sand, shingle and boulders.

Kingsand lies exposed to the south and south east, and periodically suffers damage when a storm coincides with a high tide. Recent troubles seem minor when compared to the tempest of January 1819 when 'many houses and fish cellars, along with four boats were washed away' and the 'Great Wall at North Rock turned on its side against the houses'. A similar storm in 1824 caused £5000 worth of damage. The London Inn once occupied the corner buildings in Market Street, overlooking the Cleave. Reputedly it was the best in the village until it was closed in 1910. Before a licence could be granted, an inn had to be able to accommodate both horse and rider. The London had a fine set of stables adjacent to it which are now dwellings.

One of the most distinctive buildings in Kingsand is the Institute. It is the third building to stand here since the original was washed away in the great storm of 1824, together with its sole inhabitant, a naval pensioner with a wooden leg. The two tenements which next occupied the site had to have their chimneys heightened to prevent the sea washing down and putting the fires out. In 1877, the great Victorian Temperance movement prompted the Earl of Mount Edgcumbe to purchase the tenements with the intention of converting them into a Coffee House, Working Men's Club, Reading Room and Library. The venture was not successful and the turn of the century saw it in use as a tea shop run by William Marks who had survived a boating disaster off Penlee in 1881. By 1912 the building was derelict, and following King George's coronation, there remained some celebration money which was unspent so it was decided to raise more to revive the old Institute. Work on the rebuild started in 1913, but the war interrupted things, and the new building was not completed until 1921. Today the Institute incorporates all of the ideals of 1877 and much more besides, it is a focus of village life.

The grocery store opposite the Institute was a fishermans' bark house up until about 1900 and was the last one to be used in the village. Girt beach, or 'the Girt' was so named because, before the laying of the sewers in the 1870s the water flowed down through a gulley or girt. There was also a girt between the Square and Bound in Cawsand. At the top of the beach is an old timber yard previously owned by William Carne, Baulks of timber would be brought ashore and sawn into floor, or coffin boards, in the saw pit. In later years William used a steam engine with an upright saw, and later still generated electricity with a Hornsby-Ackroyd oil engine.

The other large building overlooking the beach has also had a full and varied history. Originally a fish cellar, it had been a brewery and a tannery before becoming the local board school in 1876. In the days before radio and television were even dreamt of, the 'Schoolroom' was an important centre of village life. In the Temperance Association's Christmas tea and concert of 1877 no less than three hundred people were fed and entertained here. Prior to the building of St. Andrew's Church it was also the Chapel of Ease for Rame. When Fourlanesend school was completed in 1912 the boys moved out and in 1939 the girls followed them. For years it was the home of the local Conservative Club and recently it has been converted into maisonettes, but retaining the original shell.

Tucked away in the far corner of the beach was once one of the courtyards mentioned earlier. The houses were very old; over the years they had become dilapidated, and the court was cynically nicknamed 'Fitzroy Square'. Access could be gained either from the beach or from Garrett Street, by a traditional 'fisherman's path'. The right-of-way runs from the beach, up Duck Steps, past the Fort and over the Downers to Wringford, Wiggle and the beach under Wiggle Cliff. 'Fitzroy Square' finally succumbed to a violent storm in 1921. It was Good Friday and the last remaining inhabitant, an old fishwife named Sally Forsyth, and gone to a 'magic lantern show' in St. Paul's Church. She returned to discover that the sea had demolished her home, and most of her belongings, including pots and pans, were rattling on the shingle in the surging tide. The sight amused some of the bystanders, whom old Sal rounded upon and reproached by saying ''Tain't very funny, you know, Mrs Knapman, when a women goes to church and comes home to find that her house has been washed away'. She then salvaged as much of her belongings as she could, and went to live in Cawsand Fort, which the soldiers had by then evacuated and where no doubt she felt more secure.

'Garrett Street, Cawsand, by Roy Sullivan

3. CAWSAND

The curious mark on the wall of 'Devon-Corn', immediately opposite the Halfway House Inn in Garrett Street, marks the dividing line between the twin villages of Kingsand and Cawsand. The mark has a much deeper significance than this, for up until 1941 it has also represented the parish boundary between Maker and Rame, and one hundred years earlier, the boundary between Devon and Cornwall. The boundary line followed the stream behind the inn for a short way and then a series of hedgerows which snaked up above Coombe Park and Farm, over the hill to Treninnow, and thence by stream again to Millbrook. This seemingly erratic course is possibly due to it following property boundaries. These became adopted when the parishes were established away back in the 8th century, when the anomalous position of 'Maker in Devon' arose. Thus, it is interesting to realise that these little streams and hedges, in separating Devon and Cornwall, had earlier separated two different nations with two different cultures, Celtic Cornish and Saxon Wessex.

The Devon-Cornwall Boundary mark in Garrett Street

Just behind the 'Half Way' a small stream runs into a culvert. The stream rises from a spring at Watergate and runs down the valley beside the car park. This is where the village's own bus service once operated. Originally wagonettes, and later Haddy's buses, provided almost door to door service to Cremyll until the rationalisation of bus services killed it off in 1938.

The former boundary skirts the grounds of the Woodlands, a prominent house built about a hundred years ago. Close to the Garrett Street gate is an old lamp bracket set in the wall dating from 1871, a reminder of the times when before

1930 when the streets were lit by paraffin lamps. The precipitously steep Duck Steps, was part of an old fisherman's path. The granite steps were positioned in the 1860s to facilitate travel between the village and Cawsand Battery; before that people had to scramble up over rough cobbles with the aid of a rope. The name is believed to have originated from someone having kept ducks in one of the nearby gardens.

Cawsand Battery, or the Fort, as it is known locally, is large grey, uninspiring limestone mass which stands on a high promontory overlooking the bay. It dates from 1867 and is another of Palmerston's Follies, possibly his worst. The follies were a ring of 22 forts which were built in a defensive ring around Devonport Dockyard, during the reign of Napoleon III of France, when war seemed to threaten. The crisis passed, but the forts, which were all obsolete before they were completed, are still with us. The gaunt ugly building at Cawsand did not even possess functional merit, for when the big guns overlooking Garrett Street were fired the concussion smashed windows in the village and caused cracks to appear, not only in the house walls but in the walls of the fort itself. Not surprisingly, the guns were never fired more than twice, although soldiers were stationed there until 1920. The building was sold in 1926 for £1600, the salvage value of the stone it contained. It is a pity it was not then demolished and the site allowed to revert back to the plantation which had existed there in 1860, as its appearance has not been enhanced by recent developments.

Cawsand and Kingsand c1840

January storms 1990 — Richard Marlow

Cawsand, The Square

The Square, Cawsand, South Side, about 1910

At the bottom of Duck Steps, the Bakery was once another pub, the Red Lion, its use was changed in the 1860s to a confectioners and haberdashery. The Bistro, next door, housed the inn's stables, and then a bakehouse when the pub closed. It continued as such until the first World War when the baker, named Popplestone, was killed on active service. Bakehouses were common in the days before every house had an oven. Brown, the blacksmith of Millbrook would make an oven to order, but they were expensive, so most housewives took their dinners and cakes to a bakehouse for cooking at 2d each. This practice continued until the early 1900s when cheap American ranges became available for about £4 each.

The Bistro dining area once served as a garage for wagonettes, one of which could be converted for use as a hearse. Wagonettes were open topped horse-buses and could seat ten passengers who sat facing inwards; the fare to Cremyll was 6d. It was frequently quicker to walk because at the hills passengers always had to get down and were sometimes invited to push as well. It was mainly the more well-to-do people who used both wagonettes and the hearse. Most burials were 'walking funerals', with the coffin being borne up to Maker or Rame churchyards by six young men. The last walking funeral at Rame occured in 1933. The undertaker was Freddy Carne, who walked solemnly in front wearing a crepe-banded top-hat.

Further along Garrett Street is the old school building and it is difficult now to imagine how hundreds of children were once crammed into that tiny yard, although when the tide was out they would play on the beach. A World War II 'pill box' still overlooks the beach, and it was up the adjacent slip that the dressed building stones for Cawsand Fort were dragged. A gap existed in Garrett Street where 'Trevarna' now stands, and the stones went through the gap and up a wooden shute to the fort. On the Seaward side of the road in front of 'Cawsand House' is a garden with the crenellated wall from which Garrett Street derives its name.

Another battery once existed at Pemberknowse; it was probably demolished in 1792 to make way for the Congregational Chapel and manse. An early 19th century cannon, which was once positioned in the sea wall remains close by the little harbour, which is a favourite bathing place for local youngsters. According to a legend, a passage, a relic of the smuggling days, once ran from the head of the cove to the cellar of the Ship Inn.

In March 1917 Pemberknowse was the scene of high drama following the salving of the Orient Line steamship *Orsorva*. Launched in 1909, the 12,000 ton liner was ferrying troops to France when she was torpedoed off Start Point. The damage sustained was so serious that it was decided not to risk the passage through the Sound and up to the Dockyard, for fear of her sinking and blocking the channel. It was decided to beach her first for temporary repairs; they needed a place which was reasonably sheltered and where the bottom was neither rocky nor muddy. Fortunately the man charged with the operation was a local Trinity House Pilot, Tom Odgers. He knew a place which fulfilled all the requirements, for just off Pemberknowse there is a bed of shingle. The shingle was at the right depth and would niether damage nor cling to the ship's bottom, so *Orsova* came to Cawsand.

Cawsand Square, a wintery day, late 1920s.

The villagers were quite accustomed to the sight of passing mail boats, but to have one of the leviathans almost sitting on the beach was entirely a different matter. She was an awesome sight; her bows reared above the Congregational Chapel, and her black hull seemed to stretch away out to the Breakwater, whilst tugs and launches bustled around and divers and shipwrights swarmed over her, patching her up. *Orsova* sat on the shingle off Cawsand for a fortnight before being towed off on a spring tide to the Dockyard, with pumps and paddlewheels working flat out. She resumed her interrupted career on the Australian run in 1919 and completed seventy trips before being broken up in 1937. Shortly after this, following the fall of France in 1940, there was more frantic naval activity in the Bay which was crowded with ships after the Dunkirk evacuation.

In days gone by there were many more licensed premises than there are today. Few of them qualified as inns though, and were mere grog shops or 'kiddleywinks' with a singe tap-room. Most of them were pretty disreputable places and to attract trade some of them had skittle alleys attached to the rear of the premises. Frequently these became the haunt of gamblers and loafers and caused much concern for local magistrates. There are remnants of skittle alleys in both Garret Street and St Andrew's Street. The Ship Inn stable accommodation presented a problem, for the stables were at the rear of the building, at the base of the cliff. Consequently horses had to be led through the bar to the stables and commotion ensued, especially when farmers were patronising the pub. One such patron, William Wilton, would ride his pony straight through the bar. The scene can be imagined, when at closing time, he would be helped on the horse's back, full of liquor, for the beast to make its own way out and on up to Rame. Sometimes he went to sleep and fell off. The animal would then graze quietly nearby until he awoke and resumed his journey.

From the wall at the top of the Garretts, a short distance past the Old Ship Inn, you can look down on Cawsand Beach and the Bound. In summer the beach is a popular place for swimming and boating. My father's uncle, Albert Carne, would recall how, when as a boy in the 1850s, the third Earl of Mount Edgcumbe visited Cawsand in his steam yacht, and, being crippled with gout, was carried up the beach in a sedan chair. Naturally this aroused great curiosity, and all the boys rushed down and crowded around, jostling to catch a glimpse of 'Lordy in 'ees glass 'owse'. His lordship, who was 'a rough old dog', and did not enjoy being a spectacle, was most displeased.

"Get those bloody boys out of it", he growled and his men chased the boys away, only for them to follow at a safe distance.

The beach was a busy place all the year round, with fishermen constantly at work, repairing nets and making crabpots from locally gown willow wands or withies. This beach is less open to the south-east than Kingsand, and it was here that the big 10 ton fishing boats, or hookers, were usually beached for maintenance. Cawsand had a fleet of forty of these boats, which were manned by two or three men each. Fish were plentiful at first. According to fisherman Harry Marks, 'You couldn't drop an anchor overboard without it hitting a fish on the back', and some hake were 'as big around as a man's thigh'. The number of hookers gradually

Cawsand Beach, about 1911. Drying the Mainsail

declined towards the end of the last century as fish became scarcer and pollution increased. Disaster struck on the 9th March, 1891, when nine of the ten at anchor were sunk in the Great Blizzard which roared in from the south-east. By 1914 there were only sixteen left. The advent of steam trawlers and drifters, later in the 1920s, caused a further reduction in the number of hookers, and by 1930 the few remaining had been motorised. The trawlers came from Plymouth in their hundreds; they were able to put to sea in most weathers, and caused such depletion of fish stocks that the Cawsand fishing fleet never recovered.

Cawsand beach was also the place where most of the heavy goods for the village were landed. These varied from beer for the pubs to building stone for the forts. Large quantities of Northumberland coal were brought ashore from the schooners during the summer and put in store for the winter. Millbay, and later Cattedown limestone, which was used to build Polhawn Fort, as well as stone for the military roads was also landed here from barges. The barges would be grounded on an ebb tide and the cargo unloaded into carts, often by night if the barge needed to be away promptly. My grandfather, a builder, frequently bought a barge load of limestone, which would be dumped on one side of the beach and used as required. He would mark the position with a red flag tied to an oar. For his mortar he used quicklime and beach sand. The lime came from either of the two Cawsand limekilns, one situated around the south corner of the beach, the other just beyond St. Andrew's church.

The barges, of 70 tons in some cases, were often literally sailed by just a man and a dog and, not surprisingly, they rarely ventured out in winter. In February 1891 the barge *Providence* did risk it, and paid the penalty of being caught in

Cawsand Beach and Cellars about 1910

Cawsand Beach in the 1920s

a sou'easter. She was wrecked on Cawsand Beach and became a total loss. When her owner auctioned the wreck, Albert Carne bought it for thirty shillings. He sprang the pitch-pine planks off with a horse and chain, then sold some of the ribs to a builder for a house in Duck Street (Armada Road). He was never paid, and by strange chance the house was destroyed by a bomb in 1941. Some of the beams from the *Providence* were still in use as gateposts at Cross Park Farm in the 1970s.

At the top of the cliff, looking out from beneath Penlee Wood over Cawsand Beach, stand the old Coastguard cottages, relics of the smuggling era. They were built in the 1820s by my ancestor Richard Carne and were sited to overlook the beach and its approaches. Six boatmen and a chief officer, all ex-navy men, and their families, were housed here. Similar houses were built at Polhawn and Portwrinkle. The Coastguard also had a boathouse on the Bound from where they would launch their cutter.

Originally they had used the Slipway in Garret Street which then went right down to the beach. The local headquarters was at Devil's Point where a large craft, the Harpy, was kept for partrolling the Channel. The creation of such a force gives some indication of the scale of the problem they faced and of the Government's determination to stamp out smuggling, or 'free-trading' as Cornish folk preferred to call it. Cawsand had all the attributes necessary for a successful smuggling centre. An inexhaustible market existed close at hand in Plymouth, fishing boats which could work close inshore and were manned by skilled, hardy seamen, and farm workers who would move and hide the goods once ashore. Not surprisingly, smuggling flourished, for big money was available. After the American War of Independance it was carried out quite openly, even the soldiers from Maker Barracks gave assistance in moving the contraband. Despite the presence of naval guardships, it continued uninterrupted by the French Wars. Indeed, in 1804 the Customs at Plymouth estimated that 17,000 kegs had been landed in the village, and in 1830 that at least 81 men and 52 boats were involved in running an occasional 'crop' of kegs. The kegs, or tubs, were half-ankers holding 4½ gallons of brandy. They were imported, along with tea, tobacco and silk, first from Guernsey, then from the small Breton port of Roscoff, which was founded upon the smuggling trade.

With Napoleon's defeat in 1815, two things happened. Hordes of sailors were paid off, and having no work, turned to smuggling. Following this upsurge in activity the Government was obliged to act decisively to terminate a practice which, as well as being a major source of lawlessness, was costing millions in lost revenue. The Coastguard Cottages at Cawsand and all around the coast are symbolic of the Government's resolve: it heralded the beginning of the end. The Coastguard patrolled by day and by night, and backed up by a series of draconian laws, made life for the free-traders very difficult indeed.

To prevent the night-time landing of contraband the Coastguard kept constant watch. Warning lights would be shown, or fires would be lit and as a result it became a criminal offence to carry the means to make a light, or even loiter, within five miles of the coast or a navigable river. The smugglers then took to sinking their cargoes off shore, sometimes as far out as the Eddystone, using rocks with holes bored through them known as 'Smuggler's Stones' which may still be found occasionally, some still exist in the old fish cellars at Portwrinkle. The sunken kegs were recovered by fishermen who 'crept' them up with hooks — unless the Coastguard got there first, in which case the officers received handsome prize money. Convicted smugglers were given the choice of either spending five years in the navy, or three years in Bodmin Jail. They invariably chose Bodmin, where the jailers, along with everyone else, regarded them with sympathy and admiration. Nevertheless, many desperate skirmishes were recorded which ceased only when the carrying of arms was made punishable by death.

After recovery, the kegs would be landed at a quiet cove, or sometimes brought right into Cawsand beach under the Coastguards' nose. The beach was constantly watched and the kegs were hidden under nets, and at high tide were transferred to a tunnel for storage and movement away from the beach. This tunnel was apparently never discovered in the days of smuggling, although my father inadvertently un-covered it one day whilst re-decorating the cellar of the house in which we lived, at the bottom of Garrett Street. The tunnel had several exits, one was in a cupboard in the first floor bedroom of a house in St. Andrew's or Back Street, as it was called.

When packhorses or donkeys were used ot move the tubs, the animals were sometimes shaved and covered with lard, to prevent them being held by the 'searchers', and on being given the command 'Whoa' they were trained to go like the wind. Such were the wiles the smugglers resorted to as the trade became more difficult. Local tradesmen or landowners would finance each run, and their agents would organise both rendezvous and sales. The fishermen running the goods were hardy spirits, who, lured on by quick rewards, thought little of rowing the hundred miles across to Roscoff and back, in open eight-oared boats called volyers. The boats were normally used for mackerel or pilchard seining but this did not prevent the government from banning their manufacture, since they could out-run any coastguard cutter simply by heading up wind. Consequently a limit of four oars was set as early as 1721.

The smugglers' sailing craft were likewise very swift. The big luggers carried 1000 sq.ft. of canvas and could make Roscoff in under 8 hours given a fair wind. Those which were seized during smuggling operaitons sometimes changed role, and were used by the Coastguard to chase their former owners. Others were sawn into three parts on Cawsand beach.

Such losses were difficult to bear, and very few people made any permanent gains after 1830. By 1840 the famous Cawsand smuggling fleet was all but finished, with only the occasional run being made in fog or on a moonless night with half a gale blowing. Not surprisingly lives were lost and cargoes jettisoned. It had always been a secretive business, and now it became even more so. No one who was arrested ever informed upon his colleagues. Several of my ancestors were deeply involved, but they would never discuss it, even amongst their own family; and furthermore, in latter years, it was not considered respectable, especially if you happened to be a Wesleyan. Consequently, despite the great amount of activity that went on, little is available in the way of hard facts. The principals and organisers, who knew it all, simply took their secrets to the grave with them. By the 1880s the Coastguard was fully in control and this, coupled with the introduction of Free Trade, made smuggling a much less attractive pursuit. Nevertheless, it was not until 1920 that Coastguard manning levels were reduced and the cottages reverted back to being the property of the Earl of Mount Edgcumbe.

The original settlement at Cawsand was centred round the Armada Road-Square area. It later grew along Garrett Street, at the base of the cliff, and merged with Kingsand. The oldest house in the village is thought to be Apple Tree Cot in Armada Road. It dates from about 1600 and is a typical old Cornish farmhouse, with a massive chimney at what was the front of the building. It ceased to be a farmhouse in the early 1830s when the owners, the Trevethan Family, sold out to the Edgcumbes and emigrated to Australia. The new owners planted trees and turned the fields into a pheasant shoot.

Duck Street must have been a very mucky place, with a stream running down its centre into which all household refuse was dumped. In summer it stank. Things became so bad that in 1880 Uncle Albert, who lived at the bottom of the street, contributed £100 towards the cost of having a drain built. Immediately opposite Apple Tree Cot there was once a blacksmith's shop which was owned by some of my ancestors, the Luneys, and later by the Hockens. George Luney prospered at smuggling, and even described himself in his will of 1825 as a 'Tea Dealer of Cawsand Square'. William Hocken, his son-in-law, was almost ruined by smuggling, and had lost a brother who was drowned when running brandy to Hope Cove in Devon. 'Granfer' Hocken would often talk about how in the 1820s during wet weather, the Square would be filled with oxen waiting to be shod. In those days farmers sold horses for coaching; carts were pulled by donkeys, ploughs by oxen.

The Luneys had built a large slate-hung house in the corner of the Square in 1815 on Mount Edgcumbe land. It cost £125. Later, the Hockens, and then Uncle Albert, lived in it on a "Three life" lease. Uncle Albert's mother, who was a Hocken, was 'the last life' on the property; when she died in 1913 'it fell into hands', and reverted to being Mount Edgcumbe property. The Luney's had run a grocery shop in the house, and Granfer Hocken continued with the business along with a smallholding at Rame. He was also a Special Constable who took his duties very seriously and, as a staunch Wesleyan, had little time for drunks, most of whom seemed to come from Maker Barracks. Although Welsh soldiers were always popular in the village — on Sunday they would come down to the Chapel to sing with their customary fervour — the Irish were different. They had their own chapel in the barracks, and only came down to the village when they wanted to 'go on the cut' and carouse. After visiting all the village pubs they would be well away by the time they reached the Square, and Granfer would keep a watchful eye on them from his shop window. He was a big man with an authoritative attitude, who feared no one; at the first signs of disorderly behaviour he would reach for his mace and 'clinks'. On confronting the unruly soldiers,

Cawsand and Penlee Wood — notice the Pier

he would order them in the name of the law, to disperse and return to their barracks. He frequently met with abuse, and on such occasions would wade in, swinging his mace and tapping the offenders over the head before hauling them off to the local lock-up to spend the night. The lock-up was in the cellar below 'Marina' in Garrett Street. Next day Parson Ley, the Magistrate, would come down from Rame and mete out stern justice in the courtroom which was immediately above.

In the courtyard to the rear of Granfer Hocken's shop is a small cottage which adjoined Apple Tree Cot and where Edward, or 'Neighbour' Whittle as he was called, the shoemaker, lived and worked. Neighbour was always busy, for he was a fine craftsman, and when Bill Jago decided to get married, to 'some woman over to Mutton Cove', he ordered Neighbour to make him a pair of leather 'Wellington' boots. The smart, snug-fitting, boots cost a guinea and when the Saturday morning of the wedding arrived Bill came over and tried them on, and then set off for Cremyll in high spirits. Everything went well until bedtime came. Unfortunately the warm weather and the walking had caused Bill's feet to swell up, and despite frantic efforts, neither he, nor his wife were able to get the things off, and the poor chap had to sleep with his feet hanging out over the edge of the bed. Understandably the lady was very upset, and so, first thing on Sunday morning, Bill was knocking on Neighbour's door, complaining loudly. Neighbour, quickly appreciating the gravity of the situation, with a few deft strokes of a sharp knife cut the stitching, and Bill, relieved of his boots, hurried back to Devonport to consummate his marriage.

The 'Green', Kingsand 1935 with the Rising Sun Inn

The Cleve, Kingsand 1892 with the London Inn

St. Andrew Street (Back Street), Cawsand 1900 with the Pilot Boat Inn

Photographs by courtesy of Colyn Thomas

It is uncertain how Cawsand came by its name. Possibly it was Cow Sand, for even in the early years of this century cows were a common sight on the beach, especially in summer when they waded into the sea to escape the flies, and an early spelling is Cousham. Even more remarkable sights on the beach in those days were otters, which were fairly common around the coast. Alternatively the village could have taken its name from the Bay for a Sound is an anchorage or passage, as in Plymouth Sound.

The fountain in the Square, as is evident from its inscription, was provided by the Edgcumbes in 1870. Before this time, water from the wells or a foul stream had been used. The fountain water was piped from the meadow just below Forda. Later, taps were also connected to this source. The taps were situated at convenient places along the streets as far as Duck Steps. The Kingsand taps were fed from a reservoir at Blackendown.

The house at the foot of Garret Street, 'The Pilot Boat' was an inn of the same name. It had been the leasehold property of the Chapell family for almost the entire 19th century when it 'fell into hands' in 1911 following the death of Henry Chapell whose life was the last on the property. The land was owned by the Edgcumbes and on the morning after the death, Chapell's sister happened to be crossing to Stonehouse on the same ferry as the Earl to whom she laconically remarked 'You'm richer than you was yesterday m'lord. Harry died through the night.' His lordship made no reply.

In the cellar of the house next door was a bakehouse which had had to close when the baker, Ned Glinn, took to spending too much time in the 'Pilot Boat' and was burning the dinners and 'throwing them about'. John Martin lived above the bakehouse. He was a irascible old man who, following recurrent problems with his leg, had had the limb amputated, an operation was performed at home by Doctor Cheves on the kitchen table. When Martin died, some years later in 1913, his coffin was lowered from his bedroom window on a ladder, into the Square. Roy Carne recalled the event vividly. Harry Smale was the undertaker, and although it seemed disrespectful, he always 'took 'em out the window, so as to save upending 'em on the stairs'. Martin had been a tall man and the coffin seemed almost as long as the ladder as it was taken down and borne up to Rame in a walking funeral.

In 1927 Martin's son Bob, died. He was to be buried next to his father, but when Jack Pearn, the sexton, was digging the grave he received a nasty shock. Just below the ground surface was the remains of a leg. Pearn was in a bit of a twist until someone suggested to him that it must have been John Martin's leg. Following the operation of 25 years earlier, it had been disposed of in the proper manner, in the family plot in the churchyard where sooner or later it was sure to be re-united with its owner who was anxious to appear complete on Resurrection Day. In this case it was later rather than sooner.

The Smuggler's Inn, formerly the Cross Keys, has had its bar extended into the house next door. The inn stables were situated in the yard opposite St. Andrew's church, where there was also a coppersmith's shop and another bark house. The road in front of the church, Saint Andrew's Place, was then known as Millpool. There are records of a watermill working at Cawsand in the 17th and 18th centuries, but exactly where it was nobody knows. The stream running along the south side of the car park could well have been the mill leat, but where was the Mill Pool? Perhaps it was in the meadow above the Triangle, which was once the village midden. The culvert there dates from the 1860s, when a military road was built to link Cawsand, Polhawn and Tregantle forts. It is likely that the mill stood on the present site of Penlee Lodge.

James Carne

My great-Grandfather, James Carne and his brother Richard, built the lodge for the 3rd Earl in 1852. Following a tour of Europe the Earl had returned, much impressed with Italian architecture, and instructed his architect, a man named Perkins, to design him a lodge in the Italian style. There are many examples of Perkins' work in the village. Whenever a neglected property 'fell into hands' after a lease expired, it would be demolished and rebuilt to Perkins' specifications; the 'Shop in the Square' is a good example. Penlee Lodge is not one of his better efforts and the Earl twice ordered it to be dismantled and reconstructed to modified plans. By the time of the third rebuild, either in the jumble of plans, or out of sheer resignation, the builders left out the stairs. We can understand the predicament they found themselves in when his Lordship announced that 'It's still damned ugly but it will have to do!' So they built an external staircase, and, by the time it was finished, his Lordship was just as resigned as they were and made no further comment.

The road to Rame runs up from Cawsand Triangle beside a stream and a meadow to Forda which nestles beneath steep-sided hills at a fork in the coombe. It appears to be so named because the ancient route from Rame to Cremyll forded the stream here before making the steep ascent of Hatt Lane. The word Hatt is thought to

The Italianate Penlee Lodge

be derived from the old word for gate or roadblock. There was certainly a roadblock here during the Civil War and musketry slits still survive in a wall at Wringford overlooking the ford. The massive hipped chimneys of the cottage alongside the road suggests that they are very old, whilst higher up on the hillside beside Five Acre wood is evidence of a much earlier occupation in the form of Iron or Bronze Age hut circle remains. A hundred years ago these two cottages housed four families, a total of thirtynine people.

Higher up on the hill was Wringford Common, long since enclosed, where gypsies used to camp, and which was a barrage balloon site in 1939. Other balloon sites existed at Rame Barton, Homebarton and Wiggle, where the massive anchoring blocks form part of the hedge. The old fisherman's path crosses the road here on its way to Wiggle and Whitsands. Both farmhouses at Wringford and Wiggle were mentioned in documents of 1324, and although much altered, are of some architectural interest. Wringford is similar to nearby Trehill, and is a typical medieval Cornish farmhouse. They are built into the hillside, the excavated earth being used to make a platform upon which the house was extended, frequently to house animals.

Just beyond Wringford is Golden Bank copse; below it at Coombe are the remains of an ancient settlement owned by the Bastard family during the 14th century. Their name is commemmorated in a nearby field name Bastard Coombe. (Possibly it comes from *Bos*, dwelling; *Tarryt*, a Celtic proper name.) It is an interesting area. The fisherman's path runs up beside the stream past Coombe to Wiggle where the stream rises in a spring above the duckpond. There was once a watermill here, which last worked in 1916. It would release a great flood of red, muddy water cascading down through the valley meadows, to pollute the drinking water which was abstracted just below Forda. The steep climb up over the Hatts is well worth the effort, for magnificent panoramic views of Rame, Penlee˙and the Sound are to be had. Further along the lane the Hamoaze, St John's Lake, Torpoint and Kit Hill are visible in the distance.

Penlee Wood owes its existence to the craze among the 19th century gentry for shooting pheasants. The sport became fashionable in the early 1800s, and soon numerous woodlands were planted all over the country to provide the birds with cover. The woods and copses at Withnoe, Tregonhawke, Goldenbank, Five Acres and at Clarrick were all planted either to raise, or shoot birds in. Penlee was planted in stages; the older parts on the steeper slopes date from around 1830, and the field hedges are still visible.

It was a considerable undertaking. By about 1870 the Edgcumbe Woodlands had matured sufficiently to employ eight Wood Rangers. A cottage, Bayfield House, was built at Pier Cellars for the Head Ranger and his family. Four gamekeepers were also employed, their duties were to provide the birds for the Earl's shooting parties which usually took place during the midweek after the season had started on 1st October. The Earl, accompanied by guests, both military and gentry, together with an army of beaters and retrievers, would start shooting at Treninnow and by midday would have reached Penlee Lodge. At one o'clock they would stop for lunch at the Pier, and then resume around the Point and through the brakes to Rame Head. Hares, pigeons and rabbits were also shot, and any birds which fell into the sea were picked up by a man in a rowing boat. The whole bag was assembled at the end of the day on a wagon at Penlee Lodge. The beaters were paid, the Estate's tenants presented with a brace of pheasant, and the Earl and his guests would retire to Mount Edgcumbe House.

The villagers simply did not understand it, and thought the Earl eccentric to say the least. They would say, 'Ee spends a pound to gain a shillin'' — the price of raising and selling a brace of birds, and all for a maximum of three shoots over a section of good land in a good season. But entertaining one's guests in the appropriate fashion was paramount, even though the cost was enormous. When King Edward VII visited Mount Edgcumbe for a week the House was closed for six months afterwards and the staff put on half-pay. The War in 1914 saw an end to it all. Manpower became scarce, and afterwards money even scarcer. But whilst they were in vogue, the shooting parties were an impressive sight, and their passing marked the end of an era.

At Penlee Lodge we re-enter the Mount Edgcumbe Country Park. White Rock Quarry is in Penlee Wood, just above St. Andrew's church, and it has provided many tons of stone for both roads and buildings; the church and the Woodlands are examples. The church opened on 28th May 1878 was one of the first public buildings in Cornwall to be illuminated by electricity; it seated 300 people. In the early 1900s a steam-powered generator was used, but the venture almost ended in disaster when the boiler, an ex-admiralty monster, was being positioned behind the chancel. It had been brought in by barge, and could only be put in the right place by rolling it from the Earl's Drive. When it was half way down across the allotments, a rope broke and the boiler rolled free. It careered down the slope and almost demolished the vestry. Once installed, the system worked well, later the boiler was replaced by an oil engine which charged batteries on Saturdays until mains electricity arrived in the early 1930s.

Pier Cellars was originally an old fish cellar, complete with its own little harbour and pier, dating from the time of Elizabeth I. Pier Cottage, which overlooks the harbour, has had a varied history. Originally a farmhouse, during the Napeoleonic Wars it became a grog shop. It belonged to the manor of Rame, and it was to here in 1819, that Squire Edwards retired when he became bankrupt and had to leave Rame Barton. After his death in 1826 it was said that his coffin was carried up through the fields to Rame Church for burial to prevent his creditors seizing the corpse and laying claim to the residue of his estate. In 1889 the government requisitioned the land for building a torpedo range, and when the foundations were being dug evidence of sinister goings-on came to light, for dozens of human skeletons were unearthed. Whether they died from disease or violence was not ascertained, but, as old Mrs Smale said, "It must have been a corruptible place in they days".

The wood suffered much damage during the Great Blizzard but as the trees were relatively immature many were saved after being blown down. First they were pollarded then re-erected with sheer legs, and finally the roots were dug back in. Many survive to this day, but those cast-down in the devastating storms of January 1990 were mostly venerable giants, far too massive for salvage, even if the means had existed. They were condemned to the chain saw.

For many years Pier Cellars was manned by the Royal Engineers who launched the torpedoes down a railed ramp. Several marks of torpedo were tested here, the first of which was the Brennan of 1884 which was wire-guided and powered by a shore-sited steam engine. Occasionally one would become lost and local fishermen could earn themselves £5 bounty for locating the 'strays'. The REs remained at the Cellars until the last war when the Royal Navy moved in, they are still there and use it as an adventurous training centre and for de-gaussing warships.

Beyond the Cellars the hillside becomes steeper and is deeply incised with coves, many of which end in caves which were put to great use by the smugglers. The wood is particularly beautiful here. In the spring carpets of bluebells sweep down to the coves with abundant primroses, amongst rhododendrons planted to give cover to pheasants. Between the beech trunks glimpses of the Sound, Mount Edgcumbe and Picklecombe complete the picture. At Watery Orchard, where a stream tumbles down the hillside, old Granfer Hocken used to tell of saving wheat in the 1820s by dragging it up over the hill on sleds drawn by oxen, to the Barton. All the old saddle drains have long since become choked, and it is now far too boggy to grown anything but sedges. Down below on the rocky foreshore is the site of a former Observatory.

On emerging from the wood, the land at Penlee Point is quite open, apart from a plantation of conifers below the roadway. In 1905 Trinity House wished to erect a Fog Signal Station on the Point, but the fourth Earl, an ardent conservationist,

PENLEE POINT AND RAME HEAD

Penlee Point 1925

objected strongly, so the land was compulsorily purchased. The Earl was disgusted with the conspicuous white building so the conifers were planted to screen them from view when he and his guests passed by.

Penlee is a Cornish word meaning a headland with flat stones, and there is a fine view from here of the Sound, Breakwater, Plymouth and Dartmoor beyond. Immediately opposite is the Mewstone, Wembury and the approaches to the river Yealm, with Bolt Head just visible in the distance beyond Bolt Tail.

The scenery of the Coast Path changes abruptly after rounding the corner at Penlee, the wild coastline contrasting sharply, with the woodlands, villages and the ordered elegance of Mount Edgcumbe. As the path winds its way southwards towards Rame Head it enters classic Cornish scenery, with yellow furze brakes dropping steeply down to a foreshore of razor-sharp rocks with numerous cleaves or inlets: haunt of bird watchers and sea-anglers. A footpath runs down to the Fog Signal Station and a small beach at the head of a cove. Half way down the path is a grotto, which was built in 1827 to commemorate the visit of Queen Adelaide. On the roof of the grotto is a small seat which was made for the old men who used to keep watch for approaching mail boats before the days of radio. Chandlers' agents would also watch from here, and signal with flags to Millbay for tenders or the chandlers' boats to put to sea and meet incoming ships. It was not at all uncommon in the days of sail for a ship's crew to be close to starvation at the end of a long voyage; in which case the captain would pay handsomely for fresh provisions before proceeding up Channel.

The Draystone reef lies just off the Point, marked by a buoy. It was here, on a misty mid-summer's day in 1881, that Cawsand experienced a maritime tragedy.

Three Trinity House Pilots were drowned when they were returning to their cutter after putting a pilot aboard the steamship *Blenheim*. The *Blenheim* had been expected; the rival Plymouth cutter was cruising in wait for her off the Eddystone, but had missed her in the fog. The Cawsand cutter, *Mystery*, was on standby duty at her moorings off the Pier when the Penlee watchman alerted her crew who immediately set off in their pulling boat. So great was their elation at putting

Smugglers' tunnels still exist in St. Andrew's Street

pilot Samuel Hancock aboard that they became careless, with disastrous consequences. In a lumpy sea over the Draystone their boat was swamped then overturned. One man simply vanished, a second was struck by a hawser, thrown down by a would-be rescuer on the *Blenheim,* and was swept away in the wash, whilst a third unsuccessfully tried swimming for the shore. Despite the *Blenheim's* crew launching a rescue boat, within four minutes of the swamping, James Eddy, Henry Hooper and Edward Hancock had drowned. Two women were widowed, and twelve children orphaned. The sole survivor was William Marks who could not swim and had clung to the boat. Afterwards he gave up piloting for fishing and later took to selling teas on Girt beach, from the building which is now the Institute.

The large steps at the side of the cove by the Penlee Point were built in 1899 to enable the big guns for Penlee Battery to be landed. The first gun was an ex-naval 12 inch giant which weighed over 35 tons; it took 80 horses two weeks to haul it up from the cove on a specially constructed road, which still exists. The gun was not a success; after each firing the recoil split the concrete bed, and to save the trouble of removing it they simply dynamited it in a field adjoining the site. Three 9.2 inch and three 6 inch guns were eventually mounted in a brick and concrete battery capable of hurling shells·to within one mile of the Eddystone. Although the stairwells have been filled for safety it is still possible to appreciate what a formidable defence installation it must have been. The guns were only fired once during the last war, and then only for exercise, because a serious fault was discovered which rendered them obsolete. Perhaps this was just as well, for after a firing the glaziers would be kept busy for days repairing broken windows, and the shock of firing seriously affected springs and watercourses. There was a powerful anti-aircraft battery just along the road which was frequently in action during the war; most traces of it have now been removed, along with Rame Church Battery. The latter had two 9.2 inch high-angle guns for engaging warships; these were removed in 1929 when both Hawkins and Whitsand Bay Batteries were also dismantled.

At the north-west corner of Penlee Battery is the site of the old Penlee or Folly Tower. This was a three-sided sea mark, thought to have been built in the late 18th century by the First Earl. Possibly it was also used as a signal tower, for it was very high and could be seen in Cawsand square. Folly Tower was demolished, along with the pier at Pier Cellars, in 1914 to prevent its assisting a German invasion, but its foundations remain, at the top edge of the wood where a nature reserve has been established.

During both World Wars Penlee Point was used as a searchlight station. In 1914 the great menace came from submarines and Penlee was used to supplement the existing searchlight positions at Picklecombe, Breakwater Fort and Drake's Island. The officer commanding the local searchlight battalion was Major Kenelm Edgcumbe RE, who was later to become the 6th Earl of Mount Edgcumbe. The light was powered by a steam-driven fairground generator sited at Watery Orchard where boiler water was readily available. Guarding the installation during the early years of the War were men of the Argyll and Sutherland Highlanders for whom life was extremely rigorous as the only accommodation available was the Grotto. Later on in the war when food became scarce the soldiers grew vegetables in a plot adjoining the Trinity House gardens; the Picklecombe soldiers had a similar garden at Sandways.

During World War II three larch poles were placed as dummy guns to decoy attention from the searchlight. Real guns were mounted in 1945 to train Royal Marines gun crews but the practice was discontinued following a bus accident at Watery Orchard two years later. All gunnery training was then transferred to Wembury.

4. RAME & WHITSAND BAY

From Penlee Point the Coast Footpath roughly follows the 75 metre contour line along the top of the brakes to Rame Head. This is the old Bridle path; in the pheasant-shooting days there were to others passing through evergreen oak plantations parallel with these but low down. In the 1880s an unsuccessful attempt was made to cultivate some of the lower slopes; it was abandoned because of the steepness of the access paths, although early potatoes were grown as recently as 1931. During the General Strike of 1926 furze, or gorse sticks were cut from the hillside to fuel cloam ovens in Cawsand for baking bread (and giving it a fine flavour). Nowadays only a few bullocks graze the lower slopes towards Rame Head. The rest of the area is given over to wild life, and its rugged unspoilt beauty is amongst the most spectacular in the whole of Cornwall. The fields above the wood and bridle path have historic names: Trevethan's Ground, Quarry Park, Folly Field, Middlebarton, Homebarton and Church Park. The fields are littered with bomb craters, and Middlebarton still has the remains of the Penlee Battery rangefinder. Homebarton was notorious among ploughmen. The thin topsoil and underlying rocks frequently caught the ploughshares, causing the iron handles to jerk upwards, and many a ploughman has left his front teeth there. At the bottom of the field, adjacent to the path, is a disused quarry where the stone for Rame Church, and miles of hedgerow also, were drawn.

Rame Head — Stephen Johnson

A footpath branches up along the side of Homebarton to join the old military road near an area of waste ground known as the Dobbin, where many years ago there were cottages. The coast path itself continues below the church, and, then past a row of red brick houses which were built in 1905 to house staff for the radio station, which had replaced the traditional watchmen with their flagstaff. With the improved range and sophistication of radio in the 1920s, this station, with its tall mast, also became obsolete. It was taken over by the Board of Trade, which later became the Coastguard Service, who still use it as a Lookout. It has fine panoramic views over the south Cornish coast and the sea approaches to Plymouth. Adjacent to the Lookout is a large car park which is used at all seasons by sightseers and bird watchers. In summer families come here to enjoy the glorious scenery and picnic amongst the gorse, and anglers fish for bass off the rocks.

It is fascinating to speculate on the meanings and origins of placenames. Rame Head provides us with ample material for such speculation. It is so-called simply because its shape resembles a rams head, or must we look further? The Cornish name for the place is Pen den har. This could have two meanings, either pen meaning end or head; den for fortress; and har, either a high place or possibly a ram. The high headland fortress or the ram's headland fortress. The fortress is certainly there in the form of a cliff castle, numerous examples of which occur in Cornwall where headlands have been fortified by earthworks. At Rame a massive ditch has been dug with high banks on either side, across the neck joining the Head to the mainland. Over the centuries countless feet have eroded the banks away where it crosses the hump, but the rest is clearly visible. The tiny beaches to the east and west of the Head are known as the Eastern and Western 'Gear', which again is another Cornish word for fort, ker. An alternative explanation of the word Rame is that it derives from the old English 'rama' meaning barrier or rampart. This particular rampart however dates from the Iron Age when for centuries it would have been used as a refuge in time of trouble. A spring exists on the Head and it would have been possible for the local population to retire behind this great ditch, and have kept attackers at bay until they moved off in search of easier prey. Surrounded by rugged cliffs and with the headland refuge closeby, Rame was a perfect place for a Celtic settlement.

The chapel on the headland is dedicated to St. Michael. A licence to worship there was granted in 1397 to the Dawneys of Sheviock who also owned the manor of Rame. It is likely also that a hermit lived here at this time who kept a beacon burning at night time for warning ships. Records exist in Plymouth of payments being made to the watchman at Rame Head for lighting the beacon and for news of approaching vessels. Records also exist of a July night in 1588 when the beacon blazed as watchers gazed apprehensively down on the Armada as it passed but a few miles offshore. Over three centuries later, on a cold, wet December morning in 1755, Squire Edwards also gazed out to sea, and there, nine miles distant on the Eddystone reef was Rudyerd's lighthouse, completely ablaze. Without pausing to dress properly against the weather, the good man rushed down to Cawsand to organise a rescue party for the keepers.

Rudyerd was a silk merchant of unknown Cornish origin who chose two master shipwrights as his assistants when he built his tower in 1707. Not surprisingly the tower resembled a ship, made of oaken planks, coated with pitch and heavily ballasted with granite. It first showed its light in 1708 and lasted for 47 years until the night when an overheated stove pipe set fire to the lantern roof. The keepers were successfully rescued but one of them, a man of over eighty, claimed to have swallowed some molten lead from the roof and died shortly afterwards.

John Rudyerd was the second man to have attempted to put a light on the Eddystone. The first was Henry Winstanley, a brilliant eccentric, whose resolve to build had been fired by the personal loss of two ships in 1695. There had long been a desperate need for such a light, but the task was formidable, no one had ever attempted such a venture before in the open sea. Winstanley, however, was confident of his own ability, and to the delight of the Plymouth merchants in particular, in November 1698, lit the tallow candles which constituted the first Eddystone light. During the following summer he strengthened and enlarged the tower, finally producing such an elaborate edifice that people doubted its safety. The tower endured the winters of 1701 and 1702 but was overcome by disaster in 1703. Following a period of severe gales, Winstanley himself had gone out to supervise repairs when a great storm blew in from the south west and carried both Winstanley and his light away in its fury, leaving behind in the rock nothing but a few twisted stumps of iron which had previously anchored the tower.

The most famous of the Eddystone lights was John Smeaton's tower which was completed in 1759 and was made of stone blocks fitted together like a jigsaw. Although the tower endured, the rock upon which it was built was being undermined by the sea. This caused it to sway alarmingly in gales and it was

Eddystone Lighthouse about 1882

condemned. The present light was built in 1882 and replaced Smeaton's tower which now stands on Plymouth Hoe, although its stump remains out on the reef. Public subscription raised the money for it to be removed, block by block, so great was the affection felt for it.

Rame Head was extensively fortified in both World Wars. During the first, hydrophones with an anti-submarine gun were mounted on the platform behind the chapel. The project took over eighteen months to complete with sand and cement drawn up by donkeys. It was completed on Armistice Day 1918. During World War II rangefinders and a radar station were built there but all traces have now been removed. The Head has reverted to its former windswept beauty.

The cliffs around the Head are very unstable, as are all the cliffs in the area. They are definitely unsuitable for climbing, and several boys have lost their lives here whilst collecting seagulls' eggs. Although Rame is barren and exposed, one person did manage to achieve a measure of commercial success from farming it. One hundred years ago farmer William Wilton ran sheep, and a herd of twenty or so donkeys, on Rame Head Common, which comprises 80 acres of rough pasture. He operated a donkey hire business and provided donkeys to anyone who needed them; mostly farmers who collected sand and seaweed from the beaches for fertiliser. Boys could earn a few pence, and a free meal of belly pork, turnips and greens at weekends by drawing seaweed from Mr. Wilton. He also did a brisk trade at weddings. The bride would arrive in a donkey cart, preceded by other donkeys decorated with ribbons. The old man enjoyed some sport, provided by local lads who would come up from Cawsand to help break in his young donkeys. After a glass or two of his cider, he would take them out to Rame Head Barn, where he would have corralled a few colts. Simple riding instructions were given before giving them a leg-up:

"Just hold on with one hand on his head and the other on his tail and you'll be allright, m'son." It was great fun, for when the beast was set loose it took great exception to being ridden and would plunge and kick, whilst the old man, who could scarcely stand for laughing, would exhort them; "Big game, me boys! Big Game! Hang on to the beggar! Hang on!" And as the animals galloped away to the freedom of the common, "Well, I'm darned if I couldn't do better than that meself."

After Rame Head the Coast Path skirts the never-failing spring at Garry Wells Pool and turns the corner above the majestic Queener Point, another haunt for anglers, with the broad sweep of Whitsand Bay beyond. Following Combers Common, where abundant blackberries can be picked in late season, are two coves, Long Cove and Crane Cove where there are the ruins of a fish cellar. This was the last cellar to be worked in the area. My great grandfather would tell of earning a sovereign for a Sunday's work here in the 1850s, carrying maunds of pilchards up from the boats to the curing pits.

Immediately above Crane Cove cellar is a stile which marks the boundary of Mount Edgcumbe Country Park. the Coast Path enters a field after what must be 6½ miles of the most beautiful and varied scenery in the whole country. As the path descends towards Polhawn Beach, or Rame Sandway, as it was once

Sharrow Cove, Whitsand Bay

known, it passes behind the old Coastguard Station which had an unrestricted view down the coast as far as Looe. Polhawn is Cornish for pool or anchorage of the oxen; and I have often seen cattle wading in the sea here, cooling themselves or escaping from the flies. The old fishermen always referred to this corner of Whitsand Bay as the 'Pool' and would talk of sheltering 'up the Pool' in a south easterly. I once heard of a soldier in 1916 who came from Bolventor and went to Tregantle for training. It was the first time that he had ever seen the sea and on hearing the Bay being called the 'Pool' exclaimed, 'Dozmary Pool be a real fool besides this Pool.' He was to die shortly afterwards in France.

At the base of the cliff, which is composed of glacial debris, several springs emerge; here a local farmer once ran a tea hut which made use of the water. At low tide a broad expanse of flat sand is exposed, hemmed in by rocks which make Polhawn the safest, as well as being the cleanest bathing beach in the whole area. Despite the steep path it is a favoured spot for families with small children. The coastguard cottages, now privately owned, were built in the early 1830s and provide yet further evidence of smuggling activity. Four families lived here. The searchers, as they were called, were responsible for patrolling around the Head and along the cliff to Tregantle. The broad expanse of Whitsand Bay and its remoteness at that time, made it an ideal landing area for contraband goods. High hedged fields and lanes run inland, providing plenty of cover for moving goods once they were landed. When they were off Rame Head the smugglers had to decide whether or not it was too rough to attempt a Whitsand landing. If, once they had descended into a trough, the waves were so high that they could not see the Eddystone light, then they would sink their cargo, to be 'crept up' the following day. In the early days, before the Coastguard's strict surveillance, they would simply cast it overboard for the tide to take it on to the beaches.

The beach and cove at Polhawn are also overlooked by Polhawn Fort, another of Palmerston's Follies, which is now an hotel. The two-acre plot which it occupies was formerly part of old Granfer Hocken's holding, and he was fond of recalling how he had been ploughing one afternoon at nearby Combers Common when an old artillery colonel came by in a wagonette to look the site over. Having seen all he wished, the colonel, who was a veteran of Waterloo and had a wooden leg, discovered that his transport had vanished. He hailed Granfer who unhitched his pony and took him to Cremyll in a cart. On the way Granfer learned details of plans for another bigger, fort, and secured the land for one shilling per year until building commenced. The old solider could never have envisaged the possibility of the Fort being bombarded by explosive shells, at a distance, from rifled, breech-loading guns, and consequently the fort was obsolete as soon as it was completed. Plans for the bigger fort, which had been intended for Knatterbury hill overlooking Polhawn, were abandoned due to lack of funds. Rangefinders for the Rame Church Battery were positioned here and the iron steps in the wall are still in place.

The limestone for the Fort came from Millbay and Cattedown by barge to Cawsand. From there it was drawn up to Rame by horse and wagon, past Penmillard and the Barton and down over Rocky Hill. Great stones were dragged behind the wagons to brake the steep descent. The sand used in the mortar came

Willcock's Tea House, Withnoe Beach about 1910

up from Polhawn Beach in 2cwt wooden butts on the backs of donkeys. The sand was put in a great heap which took two years to make. The situation was not helped by some of the artful donkeys who learned to dislodge the pegs securing the sand, thus ridding themselves of their load. Boys were employed as drivers, two donkeys per boy, at a wage of 2s weekly. The track they followed has long been eroded away, except for the section at the base of the cliff which was cut from the rock close to where the tea hut once stood.

Polhawn Fort was opened on the day in 1863 when the Prince of Wales married Princess Alexandra. Everyone getting married on that day could do so at the Crown expense, and several people took advantage of this, one of whom was blacksmith Pote of Millbrook. Although obsolete, the Fort was manned by a token force of two gunners until 1926, when it was sold for £620. Throughout its military occupation the drawbridge was assiduously raised each night and lowered the following morning.

The heavy wagons using Rame Lane caused much damange to the road surface. In winter they sank axle deep in mud, and the road became so difficult for pedestrians that church attendances at Rame began to suffer. Eventually Parson Ley obtained a government grant to construct a raised footpath and to widen the lane, which was flanked by tall elm trees. At Rame Triangle the road branched off to Trehill farm. Later the military road was built by-passing Trehill and climbing the hill alongside a hedge, and at the top a drive was cut down across the common to Polhawn. The road then continued along the top of the cliff to Tregantle; a roadside stone at Knatterbury bears the date 1867. Before the building of the military road only a couple of farm lanes went beyond Trehill. One of them ran up to the site of a former windmill on the Knowle overlooking Polhawn.

Kingsand Wesleyan Anniversary Tea at Withnoe Beach 1912

Whitsand Bay

The other, Treneher lane, ran behind the coastal ridge and once linked Rame and Tregonhawke with a branch to Wiggle and Treninnow. At Tregonhawke it joined the ancient Millbrook to Tregantle road passing by way of Stone, Withnoe and Freathy. Now it is nothing more than a name on an old map but it by-passes tumuli, which include a possible chambered tomb at Treninnow. The discovery of flint microliths along its length also hint at its antiquity.

Beneath the Knowle, where the road crosses the stream is a small barn, the Rame Pound House. In bygone years, when the farm animals strayed they were enclosed in a pound until their owners claimed them and paid for any damage they may have done, plus a fine for allowing them to stray. The Rame pound, unused for over a century, is a small square enclosure on top of a bank bordering the road opposite the Triangle.

The Pound House was more noteworthy for housing a cider press than for any connection with straying animals. Penmillard and Rame Barton farms had extensive orchards, and the apples were stored in the Pound House loft, to be pressed in November. Mr. Peter Wilton, a chronic gout sufferer, was responsible for the cider press in which the apples were pressed in twelve alternate layers with wheaten straw or reeds. Cider pressing was a big event, and boys would come up from the village to watch and would suck the already much fermented juice through reeds, sometimes with disastrous consequences for it was far more potent than Epsom Salts. The juice was run into two 60 gallon slate keeves, or troughs, which were sunk into the ground for further fermentation. By habit, Mr.

Penlee Grotto

Sharrow Grotto early 1900s

The Mount Edgcumbe Fire Brigade

A Sunday in Summer, Withnoe Beach early 1900s

Photographs by courtesy of Colyn Thomas

Wilton always gave Uncle Albert, who was a fellow farmer, a cask of cider at Christmas. One rainy December day Uncle Albert, with his sons Roy and Rex had gone to the Pound House to collect the cider and were deliberating over which of the foaming keeves to fill the cask from. At that moment their dog, Sport, who had been chasing rabbits up on the Knowle, decided to join them and came bounding in, plastered with mud and muck. The dog mistook the froth for solid floor and fell into the keeve, where it swam around frantically trying to get out. Eventually it was grabbed by the collar and hauled out, whereupon it shook itself, spraying muddy cider all over the three of them.

"You beastly beast!" Cried Uncle Albert, "You filthy article," as he chased after the animal, beating it with his bowler hat. "But it won't hurt," he observed, scratching his head philosophically, gazing down at the unwholesome looking brew, "the muck will work itself out." He then glanced towards the other keeve in the corner. "Still, I think we'll try some from that one."

The Pound House was last used for cider making in 1926. In 1927 there was an apple famine and no cider was made; which caused some long faces when Mr. Wilton's stocks ran dry. However, the gout miraculously disappeared, and he never touched another drop. Three years later the faces were even longer when the press was dismantled and the Pound House was converted into a barn. Cider making at Rame had ceased forever.

Rame is another classically positioned ancient Cornish settlement, sitting sheltered at the head of its coombe. The farmhouses all have medieval origins but the cottages are about one hundred years old. Several older dwellings have long since been demolished. Opposite Cross Park farmyard, once known as Tom's Tenement, there once stood a grog shop where coffin-bearing mourners attending walking funerals would fortify themselves after, and possibly before, going to the church. Next door lived the Thomas family. My uncle's grandfather Humphrey Thomas was a seedsman and had a market garden up at Knatterbury. He introduced daffodils and snowdrops which still re-appear each spring.

One day in September Tom Luscombe of Rame Barton was shooting sparrows which were infesting his corn ricks. He was using an old muzzle loader, which set a rick on fire, and to prevent the whole mowhay becoming ablaze, the Mount Edgcumbe Fire Brigade was sent for. The Earl was justly proud of his Brigade, which, complete with horse-drawn tender and pump, was an impressive sight when in full cry. Granny Thomas was in the garden as it swept up the road with clattering hooves, rattling wheels and outriders blowing horns to clear the way, all making 'one hell of a rantacket', according to Granfer. It was very confusing, and the sight of horsemen in red tunics, wearing shiny helmets was too much for Gran who became hysterical and ran indoors crying.

"The French is come! The French is come!" She then fainted. The old lady's childhoos had been haunted by tales of the 'dreaded Boney', and 'Palmerston's Follies' had only recently been completed to keep Napoleon III at bay; she might well have been excused for mistaking the Earl's fire brigade for a French Invasion.

The Thomases always kept pigs; each autumn one would be slaughtered and salted down for the winter. These were not lean Landrace pigs, but large blacks, monsters of 17 score pounds or more. Nothing was wasted after the pig had been butchered, Gran would use the entrails for making hog's puddings, and to wash them, she would take them up to the water chute at the bottom of East Lane, where water gushed through the hedge. On one occasion farmer Wilton, her cousin, had just come out of the Penmillard gate, and, out of sheer devilment, went up into the orchard and muddied the stream. Gran was most indignant, and thereafter always called him 'Billy Tripe'. It is interesting to reflect that this same water, mixed with the overflow from two farmyards, made its way down to Forda where it collected still more waste, before being piped down to Cawsand as drinking water. This situation lasted for some forty five years until Forda reservoir was built to impound unpolluted spring water.

Granny Thomas would often recall how, when she was a girl, she would be awakened by the sound of clogs each morning at daybreak as farm workers made their way up to the Barton. There were more than ten smallholdings in Rame then, in additon to three big farms. The smallholders usually had a sideline, such-as fishing or a shop, to supplement their income. Scores of men worked on the land then, whilst girls worked in the farmhouse. Only Penmillard, still farmed by the Wiltons, remains, all of the others having become amalgamated with the Mount Edgcumbe Estate farm. A mere handful of men now work these fields — the price we pay for using machines to produce food for us. Nor have the fields escaped the heavy hand of progress. The first to be cleared for agriculture were the tiny ones closest to the farms, and gradually as more land was cleared, the fields became bigger and were approached by narrow winding lanes. Thick Cornish hedges protected livestock and crops alike from the weather, and prevented the soil from tumbling, or being washed downhill. The hedges also gave sanctuary to farm animals and wildlife alike, but they required regular maintenance, and so are disappearing at an alarming rate, to make room for bigger machines producing even bigger grain mountains.

The patchwork countryside is vanishing to be replaced by something resembling prairie. Whose fault is it? Some blame the farmers, but agriculture nowadays is big business, and farmers have to operate within a system which forces them to concentrate on short term gains, and pays them 'improvement' grants to rip out centuries-old hedges. Surely it is this system which is at fault. When Granger Hocken and Uncle Albert framed these fields they were constantly aware, that one day, someone would follow them. It must be very difficult for today's farmers to be similarly minded.

Penmillard presumably took its name from its association with the windmill and the headland, and is an old Cornish farmhouse which contrasts with Rame Barton which overlooks it. The Barton is a typical 18th century, well-to-do gentleman's residence, the like of which may be seen in any part of the country. With its four feet thick walls it incorporates the core of a much older dwelling, of which the former dairy at the eastern end remains. Rame was mentioned in the Domesday Book, when there were four villagers and fifteen smallholders with land for three ploughs, thirty acres were pasture, and ten acres underwood.

It has had many owners, but the country gentleman responsible for its present form was Stephen Edwards. He had been very successful at curing pilchards, probably at Pier Cellars, and his profits, helped by smuggling, paid for the extensive renovations which he started in 1740. Other inhabitants of the Barton had also done well out of fishing; the Trevilles, of Treville Street, Plymouth, are a good example.

The house was virtually re-built in Georgian style and re-named Rame Place. It was lavishly furnished, with attics added for the servants in 1748, but unfortunately, Squire Edwards, who was a popular, generous fellow, did not live very long to enjoy it. He died in January 1756 of pneumonia brought on by his exertions in rescuing Rudyerd's lighthousemen. Edward's successors were equally unfortunate, and in 1819 his grandson, also called Stephen, was declared bankrupt. The Edgcumbes acquired the property and the great house was gutted, and, stripped of its finer features, it reverted to its former name. The oak panelling, mahogany stairs and teak floors were removed to Wolsdon by the Bogers and the furniture sold off. For the next 150 years it was a farmhouse, and now it is a guesthouse.

Above the Barton are the church and the old Rectory, a 19th century building but containing traces of an earlier age. The present garage is supposed to have been the original rectory, and nearby is the shell of a 16th century tithe barn

The Church of St Germanus, Rame

and traces of still earlier habitation. Rame church is in an open, exposed position where the trees and bushes huddle away from the wind, and the sea is visible on three sides. It was last consecrated by Bishop Bronescombe, of Exeter in 1259, following extensions to the eastern end which included lowering the altar. There had been a church here long before that time however; the tympanum, now mounted on the western wall, and the hagioscope in the north transept, which should give a view of the altar, both predate the re-dedication to St Germanus in 1259. The name of the original Celtic saint is unknown.

The church is basically Early English cruciform; the oldest parts being around the tower, the north wall, and the chancel with its fine lancet windows. A spire is unusual amongst Cornish churches, and Rame can be compared with Sheviock which also has a broached spire. The south aisle was added in the late 15th century and is wider than the main aisle. A stone slab by the east wall is possibly part of a medieval stone altar, and higher up the wall are holes where the original scaffolding poles were positioned. In the south wall are the rood loft stairs, which in later years possibly gave access to the two galleries which were removed in 1848. The bell tower, which has dormer lights, holds three bells which have not been rung since 1945; one of them is 500 years old. Further restoration took place in 1885 when the old high stall pews were removed, although some original bench ends remain.

Rame church owes much of its charm to its unspoilt simplicity, effectively contrasting with Maker where wealthy patronage was available to make expensive restorations. Rame was never wealthy, it is still lit by candle light, and has a hand-pumped organ. The churchyard which is entered by an 1884 lych gate with coffin stone, contains headstones that reflect the parish's lack of affluence and sea-girt nature. There are numerous graves of children, and of men who were 'unfortunately drowned'. There is a 'stranger's corner' in the older section where unknown seamen whose bodies were washed ashore were buried. Twice during the last century the graveyard had to be extended because gravediggers were disturbing earlier interments which over the centuries have resulted in raising the ground level above that of the floor of the church.

From Polhawn Cove, Whitsand Bay curves away to the westward, with miles of cliffs crumbling onto a foreshore of jagged rocks and sandy beaches. On the more sheltered, north-easterly side of the cliff ridge lie the tiny farmsteads, known by ancient Cornish names, each sitting atop its valley and each having its lane giving access to the shore. The next beach beyond Captain Blake's Point at Wiggle, is overlooked by a stone building known as the YMCA hut, which for the past century has been used by the young men of Plymouth for recreational purposes. There are numerous little nooks which are haunted by sun worshippers, although during recent years the place has been plagued at weekends by power boats and water skiers from Plymouth.

All the cliff was once common land where farmers kept sheep and donkeys, hardy animals which would even graze on the furze. Following the opening of the military road to the public in 1930, farmers stopped using the cliffs and the fields gradually became overgrown. The process was accelerated when the

Rame Church, Lych Gate

myxomatosis epidemic decimated the rabbit population; now blackthorn and elder are becoming established alongside the furze, making the place a refuge for pheasants and finches.

The track down to Wiggle Beach was cut by the Fairwethers who farmed there in the 1820s. It enabled them to draw seaweed, by donkey, up to their fields. The sand being largely composed of crushed shells, was also useful for lightening and sweetening clay soils. It is difficult for us now to imagine the scale upon which seaweeding was carried out. It was hard work, 200 loads were needed per acre but the weed is rich in minerals and was simply there for the taking. Following a south-westerly storm vast quantities would be thrown up in piles, several feet thick, all along the Whitsands. Since the early years of this century the amounts have been considerably diminished, coinciding with the large scale dumping of mud from Devonport off Rame Head.

Whitsand Bay is the graveyard of many ships, and half buried in the sand at Wiggle is an old ship's boiler, the remains of the Plymouth trawler, *Chancellor* which ran aground here in a gale in 1934. Some Kingsand men had visited the wreck and had removed some articles for souvenirs, and because 'wrecking' was very much an emotive issue in Cornwall they ended up at Bodmin Assizes, but were aquitted. 'Wrecking' was an elastic term and covered everything from the mere gathering of driftwood to the looting of a stranded vessel. What it did not include was the deliberate luring ashore of ships at sea by showing false navigation lights. There were never any authenticated instances of this, neither was anyone ever charged with it in a court of law; it exists purely in the works of certain 20th century novelists and Victorian ballad writers.

In the more remote western parts of Cornwall there were cases where the survivors of shipwrecks were treated violently, but far more often there have been tales of heroic rescues of the unfortunates who had 'taken to the rigging' as the grounded vessel broke up. The local lords of the manor were usually quick to claim any ships wrecked upon their shores, although an ancient law had stated that the wreck was the property of the survivors, and it is this which may have induced the violence. The squire needed to move quickly though, because once the word of a wreck got about the local population would strip it within hours. At Rame he would be conveniently placed to safeguard his interests, although he would have had problems claiming his rights to Eddystone wrecks, which also fell within his domain. Wrecks or jettisoned cargoes provided coastal parishes with a wide variety of goods ranging from house building materials to luxury items which they had seldom dreamed of. Known as 'God's Benefits' they helped people to endure the miserable poverty in which most of them spent their lives. The Cornishman's attitude to shipwrecks can best be expressed by the old Scilly Isles prayer, "We pray thee, O Lord, not that wrecks should happen, but if wrecks do happen, Thou wilt guide them into the Scilly Isles, for the benefit of the poor inhabitants."

The best known of all recent wrecks was the American Liberty ship *James Egan Lane*, torpedoed whilst in convoy off the Eddystone in March 1945. She was on her maiden voyage when she was hit but managed to reach the shallow waters of Whitsand Bay before sinking. After the war her general cargo was removed, and for many years her mainmast remained visible above the waves; now this has collapsed and she remains, marked by a wreck buoy, a haven for anglers and sub-aqua enthusiasts. After the sinking of the *James Egan Lane* a great deal of wreckage was washed ashore, some of which was spirited away before it could be impounded. The removal of such material was technically an offence and there was much grief expressed by several people who witnessed the wanton destruction of items, foodstuffs in particular, from this, and from other wrecks during the war.

My father's cousin, Eric Marks of Cawsand, once told me of an incident which almost led to a similar grounding, in much the same position as the Whitsand wreck. It had occurred one morning in the early 1920s when he had been fishing with his father off Rame Head in a thick fog. They could hear the Eddystone's explosive fog signal sounding periodically and then became aware of engines and the persistent hooting of what sounded like a large ship moving across their bows. Several ships had come to grief in bad weather by mistaking Whitsand Bay for the entrance of the Sound, and they waited, listening intently, and fearing the worst. Someone must have been taking soundings however, for shortly afterwards they heard the splash and rumble of an anchor being dropped as the captain evidently decided to sit it out and wait for the fog to clear. Eric's father, Harry Marks, had quickly realised that there was something to be gained from this situation so they approached the ship and hailed her. She was the French line mailboat, *Paris*. Her crew had failed to hear the Eddystone signal because it had happened to coincide with the frequent sound of the ship's own siren. Her captain, eager to keep to his sailing schedule, invited Harry Marks aboard and engaged him to pilot the vessel into the Sound, where, on arrival, he paid him the pilot's fee. Everyone was happy with the outcome except the local Trinity Pilots, not only had they missed a fat fee, but had to suffer the indignity of having local fishermen knowing just what the rates for pilotage were, formerly a closely guarded secret.

Approximately ten years after the incident with the *Paris*, Eric Marks gave up fishing and went to work in the Royal William Yard. There were times when fishing paid very well but, as these became increasingly infrequent, he decided to opt for a steady regular income instead. The last 'good time' came on January 8th 1935, and involved catching a school of bass in a seine net from the beach at Freathy. His father had sighted the shoal two weeks previously, and as it made its way up the coast he had kept watch on it from the cliffs, hidden amongst the furze in case the rival Portwrinkle fishermen, or Wricklemen, should spot him. If they did then they could reach the shoal long before the Cawsand boats could get around to the beach. This had happened on numerous occasions previously, and the Wricklemen, with their telescopes, kept constant watch on the cliff as well as on the sea. After several days of anxious watching the shoal had reached a spot from which they could easily be netted, and in great secrecy Eric hurried home in the dark to rouse his father and a dozen others. By daybreak the *'Sapphire'* had towed their seine boat and larker around the Head, and with Harry Marks positioned up on the cliffs as 'huer' or caller, they were all set to go. The huer would direct the operations below, usually by signals made with a furze bush; he would indicate the position of the fish, and where and when the seine was to be cast. One end of the seine was secured ashore at Sharrow point. The boat encircled the shoal, which was entrapped in a small bay, shooting the net out as it did so. Once the free end of the net was ahore they would land the fish on the ebbing tide. It was a delicate business calling for precise timing; one mistake, either by the huer, or the men in the boat, and the fish would be alarmed and head for the open sea. However, on this occasion they were successful, and landed a three ton school of bass which they sold for £300, at 10½d a pound, a record price leaving them with £12 each after shares for the seine and the boat had been deducted.

This was the last time that Eric could remember so large a catch being brough ashore by this ancient method which had been used to catch tunny, pilchards, hake and herring. The big shoals became fished out as seines became bigger, and hookers were replaced by drifters, which in turn were replaced by trawlers. The trawlers are now armed with echo sounders that would make the captain of a mine hunter envious, and it is small wonder that the mackerel are going the same way, whilst the plaice grounds lay buried beneath tons of Dockyard mud.

The rivalry which had existed between the Cawsand fishermen and the Wricklemen was nothing compared to the outright hostility which existed earlier between the fishing fleets of Cawsand and Mevagissey. The sight of a Mevagissey boat in the bay was tantamount to a declaration of war. Another cousin of my father's, William Carne, who was drowned in 1894 off Picklecombe, was one day fishing for herring off the Eddystone when his nets became entangled with those of a Mevagissey boat. In his exasperation the Mevagissey skipper delivered his ultimate insult, ''You Cawson men is all the saame. You'm no better'n a pack of otters.'' The Cawsand fleet, along with the herring and otters, have all passed on now, although the rivalry still exists, albeit in a friendly form between the local sea angling clubs.

The anglers who do haunt the beaches and rocks all the year round have recently been joined by hang gliders, while the summer brings hosts of people, intent upon enjoying the sunshine and fresh air. Surfers, bathers and canoeists should take great care here, as strong currents carve out deep gullies where the unwary can be swept out to sea; the memorial at Tregonhawke cliffs is a stark reminder of a triple drowning of 1878. During the summer season there is a lifeguard present

Millbrook Steamboat Company buses on a summer Sunday, 1930s

on Tregonhawke beach and a red flag is flown when bathing is dangerous. At week ends the service is provided by local youngsters who are members of the Whitsand Bay Surf Lifesaving Club and are equipped with a resuscitatof and an inshore lifeboat.

There are several tea huts at the base of the cliff catering for summer visitors, although periodic storms wash them away. The first to appear was one at Withnoe or Main Beach, established by Richard Willcocks in the early 1900s. Willcocks' father farmed Withnoe. By day he worked on the farm and by night he widened the donkey track leading down to the beach, working by moonlight. He installed swing-boats with other amusements and ran donkey rides. His efforts were amply rewarded. People flocked to Withnoe to such an extent that he had to carry his weekend takings, mostly coppers in biscuit tins, by horse and cart to the bank in Millbrook on Monday mornings.

The Grotto, at Sharrow Point was another attraction which drew visitors to the Whitsands. It had been excavated by an ex-naval purser called Lugger whose family farmed at Freathy. It measures 15 feet by 8 feet and, complete with a carved poem, was finished in 1784, a labour which Lugger claimed had cured him of gout. The area was once known as West Wiggle; the grotto ws excavated beside the ruins of an old fish cellar. It is now the property of the National Trust and mercifully, together with a stretch of cliff on either side, is protected. High above the Trust's western boundary stone is a rocky outcrop in a field where there are more examples of 18th century rock carving. The western side of the rock has had a seat carved into it, above it is an inscription, '1779 F. & S. fleet pounded off. E. ran into port'.

Whose work was this? Whom was he getting at? Could it possibly have been Lugger, taking a swipe at Admiral Edgcumbe? Lugger certainly resented his enforced retirement from the navy, and was possibly jealous of Edgcumbe's success. But was he sufficiently moved to leave what, by 18th century standards, amounted to an accusation of cowardice? I can ony suggest that readers visit the rock themselves and form their own conclusions. The enemy fleet had intended to attack Plymouth (p.11), and got as far as Cawsand Bay but, due to lack of local intelligence and resolute leadership, it only lingered a few days before sailing for home.

Willcock's success at Withnoe was to have lasting results. Wagonettes and horse brakes started doing a brisk trade at 6d. a trip although 90% of the visitors still made the journey on foot. In turn the Millbrook ferry company increased their services to Mutton Cove and North Corner, bringing large numbers of people from Devonport. Later, Skinners ran buses and taxis from Millbrook via Stone and Withnoe farms to the clifftop. One of the last wagonette drivers, Mr. Jack Warren, would race cars to the narrow approach lanes to the cliff, and then take his time for the reset of the trip. On reaching Whitsand he would comment to the passengers in cars. "There! You ain't got there no quicker than we arter all, an' you paid twice as much!"

Willcocks would only permit Skinner's buses to use his route, which caused the managing director of the newly formed Millbrook Steamboat Company, John

Parson, a great deal of frustration. This situation, whereby Willcocks controlled the only access to the Whitsands, (the military road was still closed to the public) lasted until one day in the '30s when the fifth Earl was cruising in the Bay in his yacht. He was horrified to see the profusion of huts which his tenant had allowed to be erected on Tregonhawke cliff.

'The damned place looks like Chinatown!' he is reported to have exclaimed. Shortly afterwards Tregonhawke farm was up for sale and Parson snapped it up. He constructed a road up from the farm alongside the existing Donkey Lane to the cliff, and started to run buses in conjunction with his boats. The numbers of huts and cafes at Tregonhawke then multiplied, and, following the opening of the military road to the public shortly afterwards, a further rash of huts appeared at Freathy. None existed at Withnoe, for Willcocks refused to have them, but elsewhere they have become a complete eyesore in what is supposedly an Area of Outstanding Natural Beauty.

The North Corner Steamer at Anderton, early 1900s

5. MILLBROOK

Richard Carew in his celebrated 1602 *Survey of Cornwall,* gives this quaint description of Millbrook, 'At the higher end of a creek .... Millbrook lurketh between two hills, a village of some 80 houses, taking its name from a mill and a brook running therethrough'.

He went on the mention a rich fisher town of some 40 ships which had rendered assistance to the Queen in the late Spanish wars. Sheltered and protected at the head of its creek, Millbrook had enjoyed long standing prosperity throughout the medieval period when Cawsand and Kingsand were, if they existed at all, fishing hamlets. There can be precious few of Carew's 80 houses still to be seen today, but from the top of Donkey Lane, beside the Whitsand Bay Holiday Park, there is a fine view of the brook, the mill and the creek with the Hamoaze, Devonport and Dartmoor beyond. The Holiday Park now accommodates tents and caravans on what was the site of the former Whitsand Bay Battery, which in 1901 had mounted two 10 inch guns.

From the Park the lane dips sharply away down to the ancient settlement of Tregonhawke where it joins another lane leading to Stone, Withnoe, and Freathy which are of comparable antiquity. Above the farm at Tregonhawke, on the western side of the brook, are two coverts, and a small reservoir which once supplied Millbrook with drinking water. Above it are two large factory buildings, the unlovely higher building looming much too large on the skyline for miles around. In contrast the former paper mill is situated much less conspicuously in the coombe below Tregonhawke. For some twenty years the mill used to convert rags into paper. Opposite is an old quarry where the mill pond once stood; a stone in the wall is inscribed 'J. Head 1834'. This was probably the mason's name. The mill was closed before that date, following a complaint by the lieutenant in charge of the King's Brewhouse at Southdown, which was supplied with water by an oaken pipeline running underneath Millbrook from a point just below the Mill pond. Rags had passed down the pipe contaminating the brew. Evidently Nelson's sailors, who were not renowned for being fastidious, drew the line at finding the remains of old socks in their ale.

The parishes of Millbrook, St. John, and Maker with Rame, meet just below the Paper Mill at Radford where there is an old, recently-renovated farmhouse. The brook is joined here by a stream flowing down the steep hillside from Treninnow between a lane and a covert. The hillside opposite at Hounster (Hound's Tor) is equally steep and the main Torpoint road runs down into Millbrook to join the lane beside some interesting old houses, one of which has a massive old Cornish chimney at the front of the building. At the Heart and Hand Hotel the road traffic has to take a sharp right turn around Dodbrook House because the rest of West Street is subject to a one-way system. Dodbrook was once of considerable importance locally, and there are records of tithes having been collected here. In the mid-19th century there was a tannery beside the brook, run by the Blights who owned Dodbrook House. Other very old houses stand beside the road. Venton and Dodbrook Manor which dates from the 14th century.

After Dodbrook the road climbs the hill to Fourlanesend, with Millbrook traffic turning left beside the cemetery. The first building in Millbrook after the cemetery was once the school. It opened in 1812 and worked on Bell's Monitorial System whereby the teacher taught the older pupils who passed their knowledge on to their juniors. By 1840 Maker National School at Fourlanesend had opened and in 1878 permission was obtained from the Earl of Mt. Edgcumbe for the local Band of Hope to hold 'Fife and Drum' practices in it.

Below the old school lies Millpoolhead where, as the name suggests, a mill was once situated. Beneath Millpoolhead is the site of another tannery on the recently cleared space opposite the Devon and Cornwall hotel. This inn formerly straddled the county boundary, part of it being in Devon, part in Cornwall. During the latter half of the 19th century hides from local slaughter-houses (there were three in Millbrook), and from Devonport, were tanned here. Large quantities of bark was used; my grandfather recalled once how a cart, laden with bales of bark, from Penlee, capsized at the cemetery corner. Bark was alos imported from Spain and with hides were stored in the buildings which now house a garage and a builder's store. The hides were dried in the field where Molesworth Terrace (1903) now stands and the bark residue was taken to Cawsand for treating fishing nets.

Old Dodbrook

The shops in Millbrook are centred in the lower half of West Street and the Quay. They include a butcher, newsagent, draper, grocer, green grocer, estate agent, a cake shop, two hairdressers and a Post Office. The hardware store also houses Millbrook 'Angler's Mecca', the headquarters of the local sea angling club where all fishing needs are catered for together with friendly, expert advice. In King Street are a café, estate agent's, chemist and a drapery.

It has been many years since vessels tied up at Millbrook Quay. The upper end was once known as the Strand; the creek extended up much further than it does today, having been gradually filled in. In 1850 the water almost reached the site of the public toilets, where a flight of steps was used by boatmen. In the early years of this century there were a farm, three forges and wheelwright's shop, which have now been replaced by two garages, a panel beater's, a petrol filling station and more shops. There was also a livestock market which ceased operation in 1908. After striking deals at the market the farmers would retire to the Commercial Hotel, in New Street, to complete their transactions. The Commercial is now known as the Mark of Friendship and it is not the only pub sign to have vanished in Millbrook. It has followed the Devonport, Foresters, Kings Arms, Blue Anchor, Barley Sheaf, Coopers Arms, Rose and Crown and Ring of Bells, some of which have passed completely into oblivion.

Millbrook has always been a friendly, lively place. In addition to the market there was the May Fair which, no doubt shared its origins with the Maker Green

Millbrook Lake, 1905

Millbrook Quay, now the Parade, about 1880

Chapel of Ease, Millbrook, 1880

Games. At Whitsun 1783 there was wrestling at the Rose and Crown with a gold laced waistcoat as first prize on the Monday and a silver cup on the Tuesday. An interesting stipulation, made by landlord William Fry, was that the winner of each event had to spend five shillings in the house. The exact whereabouts of the Rose and Crown is uncertain but we are told that 'the back part adjoined the beach' so it was probably in New Street. As we have already learned these revels attracted immense crowds whose riotous drunkeness could not be tolerated in a society which was becoming increasingly aware of law and order. Consequently, in the 1880s, the local temperance organisations, led by the vicar managed to get the whole thing banned, a situation which persisted for ninety odd years when it was revived in the form of the Millbrook Carnival. One day, maybe, the ancient custom of appointing a portreeve and ale-taster will also be revived, there will be no shortage of suitably qualified applicants, especially for the latter post.

In 1883 R.N. Worth recorded another May ceremony; "The earliest May-day celebration to attract my notice in my native town of Devonport was the carrying of the ship garland, which used to be brought from the little village of Millbrook, and the appearance of which was always eagerly looked for by the youngsters . . . . The ship, as I recollect it first, was a large and handsome model of a man-of-war, full rigged and perhaps five to six feet long, resting on a perfect sea of flowers, and carried on a frame shoulder high by four men, whilst the customary tub-drum and wry-necked fife and collectors of the 'garland money', bedecked with flowers formed a kind of bodyguard. Practically the same party came year after year, and there was every appearance of a permanent character about the custom." He saw a connection between this festival and a festival in old Plymouth. "The carrying of a ship through the streets was one of the chief features of the feast of *Corpus Christi* in old Plymouth. The Reformation put an end to the *Corpus Christi* festival, but it was not a very great change to transfer the pageant to May-day, which continued to be kept up with befitting ceremonial." The Millbrook ship, it is suggested, was the lineal descendant of the ship of *Corpus Christi,* the chief feature of the chief pageant of medieval Plymouth.

On the southern side of the Millbrook Quay are some 18th century houses, one with a quaint high-pitched roof; behind them Workhouse Hill and Maker Lane ascend to Maker Heights. The upper reaches of Millbrook Lake have been dammed as part of a flood prevention scheme, and the former 17 acre millpond reclaimed for recreation. On the opposite side of the lake, beneath Maker Lane, stands an old lime kiln beside a pier where during the late 18th and 19th centuries, barges discharged their cargoes of coal and limestone. Seventy years ago workmen uncovered the entrance to a tunnel which extended back into the hillside. Probably the tunnel was built by the smugglers since the approaches to the Quay were watched. The Maker Church Register records the murder of an exciseman at Millbrook in the 1790s. Although Millbrook did not share Cawsand's notoriety, it was a distribution centre for contraband goods.

Further down the lake, at Higher Anderton, are a number of fine Georgian villas which reflect Millbrook's former prosperity. Another industrial relic is the

Rope Walk at Woodpark, alongside the Cremyll Road, where rope was made by a craftsman called Chubb for almost forty years. Chubb lived in neighbouring Woodpark House, but encountered money problems and hanged himself in Clarrick Wood in about 1874. The Rope Walk never reopened and now houses a builder's store. Behind it the wood graces the high slopes leading up to Maker. In the spacious days before the 1914 war, boys would roam these fields and woodlands in springtime, searching for pheasant's nests which they would report to the gamekeeper. 'Gamey' would give them a shilling reward, and remove the eggs to the temporary safety of a hatchery.

A footpath known as the Alpine, ascends the ridge here, giving a spectacular view from the top; workmen going to Devonport Dockyard from Cawsand used this route before buses were introduced. There was a pier at the bottom where Waterman brothers had their boatyard, before moving to Cremyll in the 1860s where they took over from the Ridleys. Six hundred years ago ships were constructed here for the Black Prince before his triumph at Poitiers.

On the northern side of the lake is the parish church of All Saints. Until 1869 Millbrook was part of the parish of Maker. A curate had been appointed in 1825, and a chapel of ease built, where the Mortuary Chapel now stands. By 1888 this building was so unsafe that the need for a new church was imperative. Lord Clinton, a descendant of the last lordly residents of Insworke, gave the land, money was raised, and All Saints was opened for public worship in 1895. A planned bell tower was never completed as funds ran low.

Millbrook Primary School stands on Blindwell Hill behind the church. The building had been started in 1913 but, delayed by the war, was not completed

John Parson's "Hibernia"

until 1916. It is one of the few primary schools in Cornwall built in two storeys. Beyond All Saints Church, at Higher Insworke, the road forks, with St. John's Road winding amongst the fields past Penhale and Mendennick to St. John, and the lower road leading back to Insworke and Southdown. The Devonshire Brick Company had works at Pottery, on the site of the Liberal Hall, from 1880 until 1935. Nearby, opposite the playing field, is Insworke Barton Farm.

The farm, where the historic manor of Inceworth once stood, is approached down a short lane. The influential Devonshire Campernowne family once held this manor and their private chapel, licensed for worship in 1331, is all that now remains. The chapel, today a mere shell, had been used for public worship up until 1826, after which it became a barn and then a shippen. The CEGB have recently sold the area for re-development and one dreads to think, what will happen to it in the future. The name Inceworth implies that the place was once an isolated fortification, a Saxon outpost bordering on hostile Cornish territory. The manorial farms probably included Mendennick, Penhale and Blindwell, with common grazing rights at Southdown, which the Power Station project still threatens.

In medieval times Millbrook was a thriving town and had two members of Parliament. The town gradually decayed however, and being unable to raise the required four shillings a year for the privilege, lost its MPs in the reign of Henry VIII. It is now a happy hunting ground for the industrial archaeologist, since over the centuries numerous industries have flourished and declined frequently leaving tangible evidence of their existence. The old tide mill on the edge of the playing

Millbrook 1919, note the barge of ammunition boxes for firewood in the foreground.

fields by the Football Club, is a prime example. The datestone reads 1598, but it was rebuilt in 1801 and the stone may have come from a much earlier building. The mill was powered by two undershot water wheels, with a third for the hoisting gear. The mill pond, which had possibly been used earlier as a salt pan, impounded the water, to be released by sluices on a falling tide.

At the time of the Crimean War there was a corn shortage which caused bread to be scarce; much of our grain had previously been imported from Russia, and prices rose steeply. Granfer Hocken ran a bakehouse and a shop in Cawsand Square as a sideline to his farming, and became badly indebted to Nicholas Parson who owned the mill. Parson's advice to Granfer was terse: ''You must keep the prices high Mr. Hocken. People have got to eat you know, people have got to eat.'' Granfer was unable to follow his advice, for he had to borrow heavily from his brother Daniel, and eventually mortgaged all his belongings. He damned the government 'for going to war over a flourbag', and Nicholas Parson alike, before closing down both shop and bakehouse to concentrate upon his farming.

When Nicholas Parson died his son John was only eighteen, and had to complete his miller's apprenticeship before taking over the business. As the small-scale milling of flour gradually declined he survived by diversifying and selling grain, fertilizer and coal. In 1885 he started ferrying workers at a fare of one penny across to the expanding Dockyard at Devonport. For years these men had toiled with sail and oar, against tide and weather, to get across to Mutton Cove, North Corner and later to Pottery Quay. When Parson started his steamer service it was an immediate success; but all did not go smoothly for covetous eyes were cast upon his enterprise, and a Saltash company started competing on his routes.

A brief partnership with this firm did not meet with success and the competition was resumed and became acrimonious. Both the Millbrook 'red funnel' and the Saltash 'white funnel' lines worked to identical timetables, and the steamers would race to the landings for custom, Rival skippers would attempt to nudge the opposition's boats onto the mud when the tide was ebbing, and frequently steamers were left high and dry. The situation gradually got worse; 'bumping and boring' and even ramming became commonplace, with the principle villians being the Saltash company, against whom Parson won sixteen lawsuits for damages in the 1890s.

Things came to a head on a Saturday night in May 1910. Uncle Albert was returning on the 'last boat' from Devonport in a red funnel steamer which was being raced to the narrow entrance to Millbrook Lake by a Saltash white funnel boat. It was dark, and a collision occured. Parson sued for damages and Uncle Albert, who owned eight fishing boats and understood the nautical rule of the road, was Parson's chief witness. The court's verdict was in favour of Parson, who was awarded sizeable damages. This marked the end of the 'steamer war'; thereafter each company kept to its own territory with Parson retaining his Millbrook-Devonport route and the Saltash Company the Cawsand run. Parson had won, but years of competition at cut prices had cost him dearly, he never recovered the money he had lost.

Boat Companies still use the facilities at the mill, and lower down the lake at Foss a yacht repair yard has recently been successfully operating, another brickworks was run at Foss up until 1935, using clay from the adjacent quarry. A footpath leads past the limekiln on the foreshore to Southdown, where most of Millbrook's former industries were concentrated. As long ago as 1650 gunpowder was made at Southdown; this important industry continued up until the 1850s. In the French-Spanish invasion scare of 1779 the guns at Empacombe Redoubt were trained on the mill, with orders to destroy it in the event of it falling into enemy hands. Another key installation, the King's Brewhouse, was also to be destroyed, though fortunately such dire straits were not reached, nevertheless, without any assistance from Empacombe the powder mill managed to blow itself up in 1850. The calamity did not affect the Brewhouse, which had closed in 1835 when brewing was transferred to the Royal William Yard after 102 years of providing ale for H.M. ships.

From the Dockyard's viewpoint, the Powder Mill was conveniently situated. It was also convenient for the gunnery training ship Cambridge which was moored off the Obelisk. At practice her cannon would hurl balls into the mud, from which they are periodically recovered by boys digging for bait. The residents of Southdown were less than happy about the mill, and continued to be unhappy at the stench from the soap factory, fish fertiliser works and glue factory which subsequently used the vacated mill's premises. The copper smelter of 1870 could not have been healthy either, but, since it meant employment they seldom complained about it. In 1902 a Frenchman started extracting silver and arsenic from the copper waste. Silver Terrace is said to have been built out of the profits of this venture.

The end of the story came in 1950 when Western Counties Brick Co moved out. Brick production had started there in 1888 but ceased when lime was found to be contaminating the brick shale which was excavated in the adjacent quarry. Most of the industrial archaeeology has been bulldozed away by developers and it is hard now to visualise how it must have looked in the past when the quays teemed with activity and were alive with paddlers, barges, fishing boats and three masted schooners from all over Europe.

Skinners' Car Hire, Millbrook Quay, 1920s

Millbrook, early 1900s

Photographs by courtesy of Colyn Thomas

6. SAINT JOHN, TREGANTLE, PORTWRINKLE & SHEVIOCK.

A walk which is much favoured by bird watchers is that which follows the shoreline of St. John's Lake around from Southdown to Goose Ford. It needs to be undertaken wearing wellingtons when the tide is ebbing, but it is worth the trouble for the mudflats teem with waders. As the tide floods in the bird watchers are replaced by anglers seeking the flounder which come in to feed. At Insworke there is a flooded meadow, which had been reclaimed until a bomb breached the sea wall in 1941. The shoreline twists around Penhale Creek and eventually reaches St. John where a few years ago I was fortunate enough to see a kingfisher which was after the fry that were splashing in the waters above the ford. Close by are some old time kilns and traces of medieval strip farming at Vanderbands. There has been some recent building at St. John, and the hamlet has lost much of its character.

In the 1860s uncle Albert worked at Mendennick farm, and had ploughed these fields with a team of oxen. The words he used to bid them wheel right or left came right out of Chaucer, such as *Hait* and *ree,* which came across from Germany with the Saxons when they introduced their system of agriculture. Words like *tangs* and *hames* which were part of the English language for centuries have now become lost in a world of diesel engines and pollution, subsidies and insecticide sprays.

Although the 13th century inn has been re-styled, the church of Saint John the Baptist at the bottom of the hill has lost none its charm over the centuries. The thick wooden unbuttressed tower with its pyramidal roof is unmistakably Norman, whilst the unaisled nave and chancel is 15th century. Nearby is the old Georgian Rectory, similar to the one at Rame, both in age and in the fact that the original building is now used as a garage.

Wolsdon House overlooks St. John from beside the Antony road and takes its name from the family that lived there for many years immediately after the Norman conquest (Ulveston). It is part Tudor and in the 16th century it passed to the Boger family, who owned it until 1947. From the church crossroads Sunwell Lane meanders up the coombe beside the stream to Lower Tregantle, which in Domesday had 3 villagers and 6 smallholders. The Cornish origin of the placename hints at antiquity; *tre* means farm-stead and *argantel* is silver, so it may have been a wealthy farm, or one beside a silver stream. It has also been suggested that the *tre* was added at a later date, which commonly occurred. There is an alternative interpretation which suggests it belonged to the Gandall family.

Over the coastal ridge to the south is the sea. After Wiggle cliff the Coast Path follows the road for several miles, although it is just possible to walk along the beach to Portwrinkle at low water, if you do not mind getting your feet wet at Sharrow. Anglers use this beach all the year round, and it is not at all uncommon at night in the middle of winter to see lights on the beach as they tend their bass lines. The smugglers also used this area by night time, mainly because of its remoteness and proximity to the Lynher river. There is a record of how a woman once saw a party of forty men emerge from a well at Tregantle. This gives some idea of the scale of the operations and the quantities of liquor involved; or possibly of the quantity of liquor the woman had consumed.

The strategic position of the ridge above Tregantle was no doubt responsible for the siting of Tregantle fort, yet another legacy of Lord Palmerston. Although this massive limestone structure over looks both Whitsand Bay and the Lynher river it was considered insufficient, and two more fortifications were deemed necessary, one at Scraesdon and the other at Tregantle Down, which stood beside the road where the car park is now situated. Tregantle fort was originally designed to hold 35 guns and 1000 men, but only one 35 pounder was ever mounted, in 1866; and by then it was obsolete. The fort was next used for a coastal defence brigade of one officer and fifty men, until it provided barracks accommodation for the Tregantle Down Battery which was built in 1890. Tregantle Down mounted four 9 inch naval guns, but these also soon became obsolete, and the battery was dismanted in 1905. Following this the fort was taken over by the infantry for whom the rifle ranges were constructed which are still regularly used during all months of the year except August. During both world wars the fort was used extensively as a training centre, with Americans being stationed here from 1942 until 1945. It was these troops who carried out most of the improvements to the military road along the clifftop.

The Church of St. John the Baptist

The Church of St. John the Baptist

To serve the installations at Tregantle and Scraesdon a military railway was
built, with a terminus at Wacker Quay, to which equipment was conveyed by
Admiralty barges. The rolling stock and track had originally been destined to
assist the 1885 Sudanese campaign, but they were sent home following General
Gordon's assassination at Khartoum and ended up here at Tregantle. Two
locomotives were used, one below Scraesdon, the other above; they were separated
by a steep incline where the trucks were pulled up by cable. This system lasted
for about ten years when it was abandoned, possibly due to the expense of the
operation, especially the continual dredging of Sheviock creek which was needed
at Wacker. It is still possible to follow the track of the old railway however, and
the old corrugated iron loco shed at Wacker still stands in what is now a picnic
area beside the main Liskeard road. Wacker was also important for its flour mill,
which once employed five millers who lived nearby. The mill was similar to that
at Millbrook, being worked by the tide falling from a Millpool; it was still working
in the 1930s.

In the 1870s there were large orchards around Tregantle and the soldiers were
in the habit of helping themselves to apples when returning from a binge in
Millbrook or Antony. Farmer Willcocks was wise to caper, and so he sold his
apples 'on the tree' to a Torpoint fruiterer called Hambly. When Hambly noticed
that his apples were disappearing he was understandably upset and complained,
to Willcocks and to the commanding officer in the fort, but to no avail. He tried,
equally unsuccessfully, to catch the culprits but, as he was no youngster the men

escaped easily through a gap in the hedge. In the dark, in their red tunics, they all looked alike, until Hambly hit upon a plan. The next evening he and his wife waited in the orchard and sure enough, at half-past ten, the soldiers duly arrived and, singing heartily set about their scrumping. Once they were all inside, the old man started shouting and the soldiers fled. What they did not realise was that the old woman was there too, waiting for them by the gap. As each one passed she dabbed his back with a long-handled tar brush, making it an easy task to identify them up at the fort on the following morning.

Beneath Tregantle Fort on the landward side is Blerrick or Blarrick Farm, a Cornish name implying an abundance of watercress. Blerrick lies just below the 200 ft contour line along which several springs emerge. Each spring supported an ancient settlement, viz. Carslake (which also had three mills), Trethill, Liscawn (Dawney Pool reservoir) and Trewrickle. Their earliest recorded names are Blerak 1201, Agslake 1257, Tre-uthal 1300s, Lanscawyn c1310 and Trewikkel 1348 but their Cornish names suggest that they were already long established by these dates. Blerrick was the last farm in the area to use oxen for ploughing; that was in the 1890s, and the land is still farmed today by the Matthews family, as it was then. Beyond Blerrick, on the Crafthole road at the extremity of the ranges, the coast Footpath resumes its interrupted course and crosses a stile into National Trust property at Trethill Cliffs to continue undefined, across the fields to Portwrinkle. Above Black Ball beach it crosses the golf links. I once inadvertently referred to the links as a course and was swiftly corrected by a club member; golf courses are inland, golf links beside the sea. The links were laid out in 1905,

Tregantle Fort

and my friend was justifiably proud of them and their magnificent setting. Each hole is different and full of character. Situated in the middle is a circular 14th century dovecote, built by the Dawneys of Sheviock. It was to be as far from their falconry as possible by adjacent to their tenants' cornfields.

The headquarters of the Golf Club is at the Whitsand Bay Hotel. This was built in 1911 by Sir Reginald Pole Carew in an attempt to open up his Portwrinkle estates. Much of the material for the building came from Thanckes manor house in Torpoint which had been demolished in 1909. The house had originally been erected in 1871 and, being made of dressed limestone, it was relatively easy to dismantle and re-erect. It had been the residence of the Graves family who had strong naval connections, one of which, the battle of the Glorious First of June, 1794, is commemorated within the hotel in stained glass.

The golf links are bisected by Finnygook Lane which climbs sharply up past the dovecote to Crafthole. Portwrinkle was once regarded by the people of Cawsand and Millbrook as a holiday resort. Bill Dunstone told me that when his brother Tom was recovering from diptheria in 1910, Doctor Cheves had recommended that the family go away for a short holiday, so they went to Portwrinkle. It was also a popular place for outings. Various organisations, or families would hire a donkey and cart, usually in September after harvest, and would spend the day at either Portwrinkle or Seaton or Downderry. William

Crafthole about 1910

The Old Barn and Church, Sheviock, 1820

Sheviock Creek, from Wacker Quay

Hancock described one such outing when at the end of the day, the donkey was reluctant to climb Finnygook Lane. His parents were riding in the cart, and despite repeated exhortations the animal refuse to budge. Finally, in sheer exasperation, he jabbed his stick sharply up under the donkey's tail. The result was electrifying. All in one movement the beast snorted, struck its ears up and 'took off up the hill like a Derby winner, with father hanging on and the old woman skritchin' like murder'. It wasn't until they reached Liscawn, on the far side of Crafthole, that they managed to stop the cart and wait for a very anxious William to catch up.

Crafthole was a borough in the reign of Edward II, when it was permitted to hold two weekly markets and an annual fair. It is thought that the granite cross at the top of Finnygook lane dates from this period. The cross had originally stood in the middle of the road, but after a bus collided with it in the 1920s it was moved to its present position for safety. In 1314 the village was called Croftilberwe and is thought to mean Croft hill, or because of its two crosses, Cross hill. The village was an important halting place for travellers on the Cremyll to Liskeard turnpike until the Antony-Sheviock route was completed around 1820, when it boasted two inns and a toll house. Earlier, in his *1602 Survey*, Carew describes it as a 'poor village but a much frequented thoroughfare where travellers were wont to chaff the inhabitants on account of their morals,' which were 'somewhat infamous'. The ladies of the village would then retaliate with buckets of slops which they always kept in order to meet such an emergency.

Today Crafthole has its Wesleyan chapel, which was once a school, a grocery store, Post Office, and one, much modernised inn, the Finnygook - which takes its name from the cove at Portwrinkle. There is another, a farmhouse hotel at Liscawn, which is just outside the village on the Tregantle road.

Portwrinkle owes its existence to fishing; its early development might be compared to Cawsand, where the settlement grew following the building of fish cellars to meet the increasing demand for pilchards. In 1605 Richard Carew granted a building lease to Oliver Walleys of Sheviock for a 'cellar and palaice at Port Wrickell'. The tiny harbour was built shortly afterwards, with the cost being shared between the Carews and the parishioners of Sheviock. The cured fish were exported in locally made hogsheads to Ireland and the Mediterranean, and the industry followed the same pattern of prosperity and decay as it did elsewhere.

The cellars although in a dangerous and ruinous condition, are a magnificent sight to the student of Cornish folk history, and are better preserved than any others I have seen. By peeping through the gateway it is possible to see where the fish were heaped or 'bulked' on the cobblestone courtyard, and where the adjoining salt and bark houses had once stood. The 17th century workers were seasonal; when pilchards were being caught they lived with their families in the upper storey of the linney. the outside stairway, giving access to their accommodation still exists, but the upper doorway is walled up. That the cellars are in a relatively good state of preservation is possibly due to the fact that they were used by itinerant workers as recently as 1914. these people were associated with the mackerel fisheries and worked for the local seiners, cleaning fish. The last people to live there were not connected with fishing in any way. In 1915,

Portwrinkle

The Beach, Portwrinkle

Portwrinkle Harbour Storm Damage, January 1990

men of Kitchener's Army were quartered here for a brief spell of training before being shipped across to the trenches in France. Although the building is protected, the cost of restoration by the owners is prohibitive, which is very sad, for it would make a marvellous museum.

Portwrinkle is very exposed to the south and fishing here was never easy. In the 1870s one of the seines, comprising net, boat and gear, was evocatively known as the 'Poor man's Endeavour'. The harbour enabled large boats to embark their cargoes from the cellar but did not afford much protection. Consequently the size of boats was limited by their having to be dragged up over the rocks for safety during the winter which necessitated people working together. The fisherman's co-operative was active here from the 1850s until the coming of war in 1914.

I have already mentioned the rivalry which existed between the village fishing fleets; the greatest competition over the 'Wricklemen's' fishing grounds came from Looe. If they were at sea, working over a shoal of fish, and the Looe boats appeared they would cease working. Between the wars seven boats were working out of Portwrinkle, and to supplement their earnings the men traditionally grew early potatoes along the tops of the cliffs and took them by donkey cart into Devonport market. The fish would be sold at the Barbican in Sutton Pool. I was told how Wilfred Pengelly with two companions had been caught by bad weather while they were at the fish market. It was far too rough to venture home around Rame Head, and so they had rowed up the Lynher and left their boat in Sheviock woods and walked home. Two days later, the weather having abated, they returned to the boat and pulled back down the river, through the Sound, around Rame and across Whitsand Bay to Portwrinkle. They then went about their day's work. In winter some would collect laver weed from the rocks to send to Wales for making laver bread. In the short days after Christmas, when the sun was low in the sky, and if the water was clear, they would tramp the cliffs, watching for migrating shoals of bass. By some quirk of refraction of light the fish would give the water a reddish tinge, and when the time was right, the seine would be shot. When I mentioned to some 'Wricklemen' that the Cawsanders had once netted a 3 ton shoal at Sharrow Point it was obvious that the old rivalries had not been forgotten; for it appears that in February 1952 the Pengellys had taken one of 5 tons. After the fish were landed the weather deteriorated, and over 4 tons had to be taken up the cliff; much of it was sold, door to door, in Millbrook.

Portwrinkle Harbour

From midwinter to June the fishermen would tend their crab and lobster pots, and feel lucky if they could sell their lobsters at 4½d a pound. The pots were and still are, woven from locally grown withies; a rapidly disappearing art in these days of nylon nets on wire frames. After midsummer the fishermen would be away to the mackerel and whiting grounds off Rame Head which now, alas, thanks to technology, overfishing and pollution, are almost bare.

The old coastguard boathouse stands just beyond the fish cellar, behind it are the cottages where five boatmen and a chief officer lived with their families. 'Smuggler's Cottage', was built by smuggler Thomas Helman back in the wide open heyday of free trading in 1795. There was once a secret compartment beneath some flagstones there, where two kegs could be hidden. Following the establishment of the coastguard service in 1822 the so called 'Scientific Period' of smuggling began, and many skirmishes took place in Whitsand Bay between the searchers and the free traders before the illicit practice was brought under control. The men who carried the kegs would either be rewarded in guineas or brandy, and on one occasion one of them was taken in a drunken condition beside an open keg. Appropriately enough it happened in Grog Lane, Crafthole.

At Portwrinkle we bid farewell to the Coast Footpath, which has been our constant companion since Empacombe and Cremyll, as it winds westwards across the fields towards Britton cliff and Downderry. At low tide it is possible to scramble along the shore as far as the Longstone Rock, once used by the gunners of Tregantle to range their guns. The lane climbs sharply upwards past the Coastguard and fishermen's cottages, and past some modern developments, the owners of which doubtless contribute mightily to the coffers of the Caradon District Council, but add nothing whatever to the landscape. At the western extremity of the beach is the Target Rock. On the rock cliff face here was painted a large black naval crest which the Coastguard used for pistol practice; and no doubt to intimidate would-be smugglers also. The target has weathered away now but the name lingers on although its origins have been long since forgotten by all but a few.

On the cliff to the left are square stone structures, one higher up than the other, where lanterns would be lit to guide boats into the harbour at night. At the top of the lane is the Crafthole to Downderry road, overlooked at this point be a 300 foot hill called the Beacon. There was once a semaphore station on the summit which communicated with Maker Church tower. It was from here on a showery Saturday night in July 1588 that the local defence force gazed anxiously out at the lights of the Great Armada as it drifted, under nearly bare holes, across Whitsand bay, driven by a light south westerly. Great was the relief as the Spaniards continued up Channel with Drake and Hawkins hard on their heels. There was once a mound and the stump of a mast here, but it is now gone. The view, however, remains and is breathtaking, with the sea on one flank and St. German's creek and Sheviock woods on the other, and the Rame peninsula and Devonport stretching away to the eastwards. In the foreground Crafthole sprawls along the ridge to Sheviock, and it is here that we must go to end our journey.

We leave Portwrinkle by way of Sanders' Lane, a long green tunnel of high

14th Century Dovecot, above Portwrinkle .

hedges and storm-bent trees, which leads directly inland from the golf club car park. Presumably the Sanders were farm workers of bygone years who used the lane to take beach sand to the fields for fertiliser (alternatively 'Sanders' is Cornish dialect for the hedge plant Alexanders). As we have seen, this was common practice all along the coast, and inevitably donkeys were used. At Portwrinkle the donkeys carried canvas-lined pannier baskets, called dorsels, and their immense contribution to agriculture is commemorated by the abundance of Donkey Lanes which exist, not least in Portwrinkle itself.

Sanders' Lane has been the subject of a Green Lanes clearance project. It climbs from the car park to Downderry road before descending the far side of the coast ridge to join Trewrickle lane just below Trewrickle farm. The farm is the historic settlement mentioned in 1135, from which the name Portwrinkle is derived. As will be recalled, the fish cellars were built at Portwrickell and, leased from the Carew family. Just below the lane junction is a withy garden where willow wands are still grown for crab pot making. Another Green Lane leads from beside the garden to Dunn Hill, Tredrossel and Polscoe (Cornish, *pol*, pool; *scaw*, elder trees) where there was once a water mill. By turning right at each junction it is possible to make a circular trip and return to Portwrinkle by way of Stumpy Cross (Crafthole's second granite cross), Pool farm (associated with the Pole family), Trewrickle and Donkey Lane. In all it is a delightful walk, from low sea cliffs through a picturesque coombe amidst rounded wooded hills and back again with nothing but songbirds for company.

At Stumpy Cross, Trewickle Lane continues along Horse Pool to Sheviock. After seeing the rampant development which has so blighted other villages in this locality, Sheviock is a joy to visit. The village is a typical Cornish churchtown and is unspoilt, despite it being bisected by the main Liskeard road. As with any churchtown, the church is its focal point. At Sheviock we have a beautiful Early English style building which bears a close resemblance to Rame, but constrasts sharply in its situation. Rame, high and exposed, has trees huddling away from the wind; but Sheviock is in a soft, sheltered valley where the trees grow straight and are blossom covered in spring. The fine octagonal broached spire at Sheviock is more elegant and less weathered than Rame's, but the two are so strikingly similar that it has been suggested that they were fashioned by the same hands. On the tower's west wall is a merchant's head, but whether it is a portrait of the mason or benefactor is unkown.

Sheviock church was dedicated to Saints Peter and Paul on the 13th October 1259 by Bishop Bronescombe, when he travelled his diocese from Exeter on a tour of consecration and re-dedication following a period of rapid church expansion. On the following day he was at Antony, and on the day after that (15th), Rame; all told he visited some 30 parishes over a period of three months, quite an expedition in those days. At Sheviock the church had been extended eastwards, with a new site provided for the high altar which necessitated the re-consecration. The tower, nave, chancel and font are all the fabric remaining of this period, although it is certain that a much older Saxon or Norman church had existed here long before, since Sheviock is mentioned in Domesday. The

Medieval Cross, Crafthole

sedilia (sitting places) and Early English windows on the right also date from this period, and the east window contains lancet lights and bar tracery. North and south transepts were added in the 14th century; the church remained in the cruciform pattern until about 1430, when the northern side of the building was altered and a new aisle built. The old north transept window was retained and was built into the west wall of the aisle, where it remains today.

Effigies are rare in Cornish churches. Those at Sheviock are believed to be those of Sir Hugh Courtney, his son Edward and his wife, who all died between 1370 and 1375. They were the Earls of Devon who were active during the Hundred Years War; Sir Edward was believed to have been killed in France and his body brought back for interment. Sir Hugh's wife was Emmeline Dawney, and it was she who was largely responsible for the church extensions and the building of the old tithe barn. The northern effigy was removed and repositioned during these operations when pews were first provided; several of the carved bench ends survive to this day. Late in the 19th century the church underwent a drastic restoration which included re-roofing and re-flooring. The churchyard was also extended; when graves were being dug they found 'bones going in all directions'. Points of interest in the church include the hagioscope and stocks in Dawney aisle, and the family coat of arms which consitutes a fragment of stained glass in the window nearest the pulpit and which dates from 1370. In addition there are rood loft stairs and a piscina. It is also noticeable that several of the pillars supporting the aisle are several degrees from the vertical; whether this is by accident or design is unknown.

Sheviock has three rectory buildings. The oldest, Glebe House, dates from 1680 and has been carefully restored in beautiful gardens neighbouring the churchyard. The Victorian rectory dates from 1845, and the current home of the incumbent dates from 1970. There is also a fine row of Elizabethan cottages which are crowned by a new square red brick chimney stack, and the Cote farm which was mentioned in the registers of 1607. The registers contain much interesting information, for example, in 1715 a congregation of many hundreds gathered to witness the baptism of a negro servant; such an event always drew large crowds.

The row of houses adjacent to the church on the main road are also rich in history. In the garden wall of the end house which is also the churchyard wall, are niches called 'bee-boles' where bee keepers put their woven raffia bee skips. The middle house was once an inn, the Carew Arms, which was very popular a century ago. For too popular for its own good, in fact, for church attendances were adversely affected by the competition. When the bell ringers started trooping out after ringing without attending the services, it was the last straw. The rector Mr. Glanville, a man of resolution as well as substance, took the only course open to him. He bought the pub and closed the place down. The 1875 photograph shows it just before its closure, the landlord and his brother, the postman are standing outside.

Close by is the old toll house, a remnant of the old Torpoint to Liskeard turnpike. When animals from the Glebe (church) farm were being moved they would be led by a circuituous route through the fields to avoid passing the toll house. The

The Old Rectory, Glebe House, Sheviock, today

Effigies, Sheviock Church

Glebe Barn, next door, has now been tastefully converted into a guest house. It had been used as a tithe barn after the old barn roof fell in, and for many years Harold Dawe ran a corn threshing business from here. It was a familiar sight, during the winter months, to see the great threshing machine being towed around to the farm rickyards by a steam traction engine. The machine became redundant in the 1960s with the advent of the combine harvester, but its remains can still be seen, quietly rusting away at nearby Berry Down on George's Lane. Just below Trethill, where an Iron Age burial was discovered, is the site of a holy well, the Lady Well.

Sheviock Church

The Barton farm stands opposite the church and is believed to occupy the site of the Dawney's 1330 crenellated manor house. The tithe barn stood next to it and, according to Carew, cost three halfpence more to build than did the church, evidently a story which he relieved since 'it is a great barn and a small church'. After the roof fell in in 1836, it gradually decayed until the 1930s when the present barn was built.

Our last port of call in Sheviock is George's Quay, and it is appropriate that we should end this book where we began it, beside a river. Our journey began beside the busy Tamar at Cremyll, and it will end at a forgotten landing beside what is Cornwall's forgotten, but possibly loveliest river, the Lynher. Lynher in Cornish means 'long lake'; and at high water here it looks exactly like one with neither estuary nor source visible.

The Quay has now disappeared; it once stood at the end of George's Lane which runs from the west gate of the churchyard due north to the river, a distance of about 1km, just over half a mile. From the church, take either the route skirting Glebe House garden, or the one running past the old school. The routes soon join and climb the hill to Berry Down, where there are the remains of an Iron Age earthwork. The name Berry *(Bury)* suggests a Saxon presence, and Pendean *(Pen,* head; *dun* or *dinas,* fort), also indicates an earlier Celtic occupation. The lane next dips down in to the wood, where smugglers once hid their brandy before moving it across to Erth and Saltash. Pheasants are still reared here and a part-time gamekeeper is employed. The lane becomes very muddy, with side tracks leading off for forestry vehicles, but runs straight down to the water. The final thirty yards are rugged going; but the effort is worthwhile, for at this point the scene is quite idyllic. The stretch below where the Lynher joins the Tiddy is sometimes called St. German's river, a broad expanse of water, peaceful and silent. Looking out from under the thickly wooded slopes at St. George's, Erth hill rises on the far side of the river; and sweeping around on the left is Dandy Pool (famous for salmon), St. Germans, the river Tiddy and Tideford (which my grandfather always pronounced 'Tiddyford'). On the right, downstream around the bend is Ince Castle, Antony, Saltash and Devonport. The tranquility is interrupted only by the haunting cries of the wildfowl and gulls, though at weekends they are joined by the occasional pleasure craft chugging by. But it was not always so deserted, and, like so many other places in this forgotten landscape, is haunted by the ghosts of earlier times.

There was once a ford here, across to Erth, and possibly a ferry also, but the most important function of George's was a landing place. Cornish, Saxons and Normans came ashore here not to mention the Celts of Berry Down, and it continued to be in use well into the present century. In Cornwall the waterways, both inland and coastal, have from the earliest times been the most important thoroughfares. Steep hills and boggy valleys made transport overland difficult, and so where ever possible people and goods were moved by water. For centuries the Lynher was the route by which ore from the lead mines, stone from the numerous riverside quarries and agricultural produce were exported. Sailing barges were used; in latter years they became motorised. On return jouneys they would

Old Cottages, St. John, at the turn of the century, the Country Carpenter's house

St John

St John

Crafthole   *Photographs by courtesy of Colyn Thomas*

Portwrinkle Harbour 1907

Carew Arms Sheviock 1878

bring coal and limestone. The barge skippers were usually local men who knew the river, with all its numerous mud banks, tides, and currents. They would call in at George's to drop off and pick up, passengers, produce, and at one time bricks from one of Sheviock's 19th Century brickworks. Given the present neglected state of George's Lane, one would never suspect that it was once such an important link with the outside world.

The completion of the turnpike through Wacker in the 1820s and the gradual improvement in roads together with the Great Western Railway, caused the river to go into decline as a commercial route. Ironically it contributed to its own demise, for much of the stone carried in its latter years was roadstone, the 'blue elvan trade', as the barge skippers termed it, from the quarries at Treluggan and Poldrissick. The decline of Devonport Market, started by the amalgamation of the Three Towns, aided by Hitler's war, and completed by the Dockyard expansion, brough the end. The market boats which were the last to call at George's, and had clung to their existence up until the 1930s, finally disappeared, and the lane was abandoned to the elders and the oaks. George's Quay has turned full circle, and must look much the same now as it did before men's feet trod the slopes of Berry Down.

Appendix 1.

SEA — ANGLING

The coastline between Seaton and Wilcove offers a greater variety of sizable specimens to the angler than anywhere else in the south west of England. Not surprisingly, the area supports a flourishing angler's club promoting weekend contests, which, even in the depths of winter, can attract over 200 anglers.

Whitsand Bay has what must be the best bass-fishing beaches in the country; here, in recent years, complete novices have taken fish of over 15 and 13lbs. The success of the beach is due to its open south-westerly aspect, whereby rough seas stir the sea bottom feed which attracts the hungry fish. Not only are record breaking bass caught, but a 15lb huss (dogfish), and a 7½lb wrasse, were recently taken at Downderry and Portwrinkle respectively.

One local skin diver holds the unique record in catching two turbot, both over 20lb in 1960 and in 1983 at Polhawn in only ten feet of water, the fish were over 1½ feet in diameter and had ten inch mouths. A further sobering thought for swimmers was the capture of a 42lb conger eel from one of the bathing beaches.

Queener Point and Rame Head provide excellent fishing for wrasse, pollack, bass and mackerel, although the bottom is deep and rugged and takes a heavy toll of gear. Rame Head is one of the only two places in the country where bass used to shoal within casting distance of rock anglers. The fish were accompanied by flocks of gulls which would dive into the shoal of sprats and sand eels forced to the surface as they tried to escape the attentions of the bass, and often of mackerel also. Alas, those days appear to have gone for ever following the indiscriminate laying of monofilament nylon nets all along the coastline, and at the Eddystone breeding grounds in particular. Conger and garfish feed at night, and big specimens are often taken by night anglers at the Head. Low river levels have also resulted in salmon being taken during the summer months.

The rocks between Rame and Penlee are also popular for bass, wrasse and mackerel. Occasionally pollack of over 10lbs are taken here, and there are also tales of giant conger eels which lurk in the gullies of the Draystone just off the Point. These fish have sometimes been hooked by boats at night time, only to be cut free by the terrified anglers after the fish have broken the surface. Having seven feet of fighting, writhing, jaw-snapping conger in a small boat is no joke, especially when there is only a dim torch for illumination. One such Draystone monster was reliably estimated as being over ten feet in length, and swallowed four feet of another fish with ease. And it is still there.

In March every year plaice fishermen are attracted to Cawsand beach; whilst the bay can provide dabs, pollack and whiting from boats. The rocks towards Picklecombe are good for mullet and the tide rip between Drake's Island and the Breakwater is a popular area for drift fishing for bass although the increase in river pollution has much diminished catches recently. The deepest part of the harbour is Barn Pool; large conger may be found amongst the debris on the sea bed there, and also in the area off the pontoon at Looking Glass Point, Wilcove.

Also, in spring time, attention focusses upon Cremyll beach where thornback ray up to 18lbs are not uncommon.

Very occasionally angler fish of up to 50lbs make their way inshore from the deeps and enter the river. It seems that they do this when they are about to die; they can becomre trapped in the pools at Cremyll and at Ferry beach Torpoint.

Southdown and St. John's Lake are well known as winter flounder fishing grounds, with 3½lb fish sometimes being taken in only a few inches of water. Quite often big fish become trapped here in mud hollows by an ebbing tide, and large pollack, cod and salmon are taken. The Millbrook and Southdown mudflats also provide fishing bait in the form of lug and rag worms, although they may be obtained in Millbrook together with all other angler's requirements.

Appendix II.

BIRD WATCHING ON THE RAME PENINSULA

The Rame Peninsula holds a wide variety of types of habitat. It lacks any natural medium or large areas of fresh water and a significant fresh water marsh area. Probably of greatest importance to most bird watchers are the coastal stretch, an important landfall for migrants and for watching seabirds, and the extensive sheltered estuarine areas.

Aquatic Habitats

1. The mudflats and gullies of the Lynher and St. John's Lake:
   From end of July look for waders in 'funny' plumages returning from breeding grounds. Through Autumn and Winter also dabbling and diving ducks and grebes. Occasional Brent Geese, divers. Almost annual Spoonbill. Flock of Canada Geese. Regular wintering Pintail, Greenshank and Spotted Redshank. At these places, and at Millbrook, search gull flocks carefully for Mediterranean and Ring-Billed Gulls.

2. The waters of the Hamoaze, The Sound and Cawsand Bay:
   Cormorants and the commoner gulls all year. After storms can hold 'odd' sea birds. Leach's petrels have been seen as far up the Tamar as Cargreen! Several species of terns on passage, Grebes, divers, auks.

3. Coast from Penlee westwards:
   With a telescope, a great place for sea-watch. Skuas, Gannets, auks, shearwaters, Kittiwakes, Fulmars, petrels, sea ducks . . . and hunting Peregrines. Choose your weather conditions with care. Then there's Spring migration. They all seem to make for Rame when the weather's right for a crossing from France. Many unforgettable early mornings here when every bush seems to hold a warbler, swallows and martins sail gratefully in from the south . . . even the possibility of Turtle Doves in the sycamores at Penlee. Then a little later the Swifts came screaming in. Pity that the fascinating/infuriating years of searching the gorse-covered slopes for the breeding of Dartford Warblers seem to be past. Also a pity that the Choughs didn't find Tregonhawke to their liking! You never know what you'll find. Even if there seem to be birds around, what wonderful views! Autumn even brings the possibility of American visitors. Anything's possible, after that Wilson's Warbler at Rame Barton in October 1985.

Land Habitats

1. Parkland and Open Woodland at Mount Edgcumbe.
2. Hedges and Scrub.
3. Belts and patches of woodland, some bordering creeks.
4. Gorse-covered cliff slopes at Penlee, Rame and Whitsand Bay.
5. Open fields.
6. Old farm buildings . . . sadly getting fewer!

The widest variety of land birds will be seen during the Spring migration in March and April. When weather conditions have kept birds pinned down on the continent, then the conditions make a crossing possible, the early morning 'falls' of Summer visitors at Rame/Penlee can be very memorable. Then there are those May mornings when the arriving Swifts, having probably spend every minute since last August on the wing over Africa, come screaming over your head 'hoovering' up the insect protein in preparation for a brief breeding season. They'll be gone again in August! Make the most of the Summer.

In Spring watch out for Ring Ouzels, Greenland Wheatears on their journey to Canada, Redstarts, Winchats, Grasshopper Warblers, Whitethroats may even stay in the gorse to breed. Then there are the 'residents' like Yellowhammers, Linnets, Stonechats, Dunnocks, Kestrels and Buzzards, Jackdaws, Carrion Crows, Ravens, Cormorants hang out their wings on the rocks near the tide-line, Herring Gulls' yells echo around Queener and Amory Bight, Fulmars shear around Rame, Oystercatchers pipe among the lower rocks for most of the year. 'Flat-topped' Sandwich Terns rest on the de-gaussing buoys in late Summer or raucously chase the shoals of sand eels.

Gannets circle and dive between you and the Eddystone, or beat across the waves heading along the Channel, the adults flashing a silver-white contrasting with the dark youngsters. Neat Kittiwakes in groups fly purposefully, keeping clear of the coast in this area, Black and white Guillemots or Razorbills flap wildly along the troughs of waves or bob like corks between dives, specks in the distance. Manx Sheerwaters flap and glide stiffly, black contrasting with white as they bank and wheel. That sheet of water between you and the lighthouse may look empty of bird-life, but rarely is.

If you really fancy your chances, try sorting out the various gulls in their multiplicity of plumages at Millbrook. Never a dull moment for the cryptographer.

A walk through Mount Edgcumbe Park for some gently bird-watching sheltered from the windy excesses of the coast. Plymouth always looks better from here too! This is the area for woodland birds . . . even Long-tailed Tits and Nuthatches in cork oaks. There's a fair population of Jays here. Great Spotted and Green Woodpeckers can be seen, and heard . . . and it's difficult to walk through the park without at least a glimpse of the deer.

Bob Hannaford,
11th February, 1990.

Appendix III.

WILDLIFE DISCOVERY: PAST AND PRESENT

Within our 'forgotten corner' naturalists have found rich pickings over the years and quite unusual discoveries are still being made today. The heyday of natural history collecting was the 18th and 19th centuries, whether birds, plants or insects. Today cameras and other sophisticated optical equipment have replaced the gun and cabinets of specimens but our wildlife now faces much greater threats in the form of pollution and habitat destruction, through hedgerow grubbing, the filling-in of small ponds, the felling of woodland and the creation of housing estates and marinas.

One of the most notable historic visitors to the area was the great early botanist John Ray of Cambridge who passed through on a botanical tour of Devon and Cornwall on 5th July 1662. His most exciting find was the very rare Field Eryngo just opposite Cremyll at Devil's Point (where it still grows today, over 300 years after he noted it!) On 27th June 1845 the Rev. William Hore added the parasitic Carrot Broomrape to the British list after its discovery at Whitsands; it still occurs locally along the coast, most notably at Portwrinkle, but in few other places in Britain. In 1867 the Greater Burnet Saxifrage was found at Cawsand by Isaac Keys, a Devonport bookseller and printer, it is now known to be frequent in hedges between Millbrook and Wiggle, but apart from the Rame peninsula and a couple of spots near Saltash it is unknown elsewhere in Cornwall.

The greatest contribution to be made to our flora was to come a little later when Thomas Archer Briggs of Egg Buckland published his 'Flora of Plymouth' in 1880. Briggs was one of the most discerning field botanists that this country has ever produced and corresponded and exchanged specimens with many of the most famous botanists of his time, not only in this country but throughout Europe. Briggs combed the Rame peninsula and came up with many exciting finds, over 100 years later we still have several growing where he found them, others sadly have long gone. He added the Plymouth Pear to the British list in 1875 which he first noted at Egg Buckland (they still grow there surrounded by industrial estates), a few years later he found a very old bush near Higher Tregantle and 3 more to the west of Seaton; the Tregantle bush was still present in 1932 but has not been found since and nobody has been able to refind the Seaton bushes. Interestingly enough no more Plymouth Pears were found in Britain until 1989 when a bush was discovered in an old hedge near Truro. In the same year Briggs added yet another plant to the British list, the Shore Dock (one of the world's rarest docks), which he found scattered along our beaches but today it only grows at Polhawn; two other national rarities, the Hairy and the Slender Birdsfoot Trefoils grow in several Places along the coast and are perhaps more widespread then they were in his day. Notable botanical finds are still being made in the district, in 1987 several patches of Grass-leaved Orache were located by Ray Gould along the shore of Millbrook creek (the one previous Cornish record being from Par) and in 1989 a plant new to Britain was found, but for the sake of the plant its identity and the site are being kept 'quiet'.

A total of 257 bird species have been recorded from the parishes, with 78 of these breeding. This number reflects the high number of migrant birds that pass through our coastline and estuaries. Thousands of non-breeding wading birds and gulls frequent the estuaries, with St John's Lake being one of Cornwall's most important sites, it is designated a Site of Special Scientific Interest (SSSI). Sadly over the past 25 years we have witnessed considerable declines in numbers of certain species using our mudflats, number of Knot, Black-tailed Godwit, Widgeon and Mute Swan have declined by about 75 per-cent for reasons that are still unclear. Others have remained quite stable with Dunlin Being the most abundant wader, having a regular mid-winter peak of 4000 making it a site of national importance to them. Millbrook supports some 10-15 Greenshank in winter and Wacker holds 15-20 Spotted Redshanks, ranking these places a nationally important wintering sites. It is sad to report the loss of three rare breeding birds from the area, Cirl Bunting, Wood Lark and Dartford Warbler, all gone in the past ten years; the first two were quite numerous even in the 1960s, again reasons for their demise are still uncertain. One of the most spectacular finds recently was a pair of Choughs at Treganhawke in the autumn of 1986, the birds spend five months in the area but sadly one picked up an infestation of the parasitic gape-worm and died, the other soon disappeared. The last original Cornish Chough had died of old age over 10 years previously on the north coast and it is presumed that our birds had come from Wales where they are still quite numerous on the coast. Hopes of having them back naturally as a living emblem of the country were however raised by our birds. Research continues through the Operation Chough project to find out the reasons of the original disappearance of our most evocative crow.

In Victorian times a number of the gentry collected birds, and taxidermy was a respected and skilled trade, our local taxidermist was Pincombe of Devonport. For the sake of a few pennies many unusual birds were brought to him by the local 'peasantry' and sold at inflated prices to collectors. Interesting local records included a Snowy Owl killed by a boatman on St John's Lake in 1838. St. John's Lake was also said to have been the location where a Calandra lark was killed in August 1863; it would have been a new bird for Britain but it has never been accepted as by then Pincombe was suspected to be not above importing the odd foreign bird to sell at high prices as locally 'obtained'. However to give him his due he advertised the specimen as the less rare Shore Lark and clearly had no idea of its true identity, so it may well have been a genuine record. It was not until October 1985 that our district was to produce a proven ornithological 'first for Britain' when a Wilson's Warbler was located by Roger Smaldon in the lane by Rame church to stay only a few hours to give a handful of lucky birdwatchers a sight they will never forget, it was photographed and provided the first and only record of this bird away from the Americas. It had turned up in the wake of hurricane 'Gloria' and was quickly followed by Britain's ninth Parula Warbler, discovered by Ray Gould at Penlee Point a few days later. A Forster's Tern that spent a week on the Lynher in October 1982 after being found by Steve Madge at Wacker was Britain's second record, the first had been at Falmouth only two years earlier.

Entomologists have also worked the area quite well, with perhaps the most interesting habitat being the frost-free zone along the foot of the cliffs. Way back in the 1850s a tiny day-flying moth, the Thrift Clearwing, was discovered for the first time in Britain at Whitsand Bay by J. J. Reading, it still occurs along the cliffs there but it takes a practised eye to spot it as it flits amongst the thrift clumps. A number of rare resident moths have been discovered by running light traps in recent years along the coast. The west beach at Portwrinkle has been the most productive (perhaps because it is so accessible) with such scarce species as the Black-banded, Hoary Footman, Devonshire Wainscot, Beautiful Gothic and Barrett's Marbled Coronet coming to light. Migrant species too occur regularly in summer and autumn, but although a number of rare insects turn up every year few can match the excitement of late October 1988 when a Saharan dust storm deposited Desert Locusts across parts of southern Britain, locally we had them reported from Millbrook, Torpoint and Tregantle and associated with this was an African Saddleback Dragonfly found alive, but moribund, at Mount Edgcumbe by Ian Berry.

Dolphins and Porpoises were until relatively recently a not unusual sight off our coast but today they are a rare event, and most recent occurrences have referred to dead animals washed ashore rather than live sightings. Killer Whales have occasionally been sighted from fishing boats in Whitsand Bay and 3 were sighted from Rame Head in May 1984. The close proximity of the gulf stream brings a few Basking Sharks to Whitsand Bay every summer, but they are rarer than they used to be; this warm water current drifts the occasional surprise from tropical waters, for example a dying half-ton Leathery turtle was washed up at Tregantle 27th December 1983 and Clive Pope and Mark Treays found a very strange fish dead at Freathy on 7th February 1987, luckily it was photographed and eventually identified by the British Museum as a Smooth Pufferfish, the first British record.

Our sea and estuary life is also well-documented, we are fortunate to have the headquarters of the Marine Biological Association of the United Kingdom at Plymouth, their publication 'Plymouth Marine Fauna' has been published and revised three times, the latest unfortunately way back in 1957. This impressive book lists all marine creatures recorded in the area.

The Caradon Field and Natural History Club publishes an annual summary of the most interesting wildlife observations made in the area. Readers are recommended to consult their publications for information on the species likely to be encountered. Details from Steve Madge, 2 Church Row, Sheviock.

Steve Madge
January 1990

Appendix IV.

SOME PLACE NAMES OF THE RAME DISTRICT
and suggested interpretations

Cawsand	Couysson 1404; Causam Bay 1602 (Carew)
Crafthole	Croftilberwe 1314; Old English croft, paddock + holh, hollow (Cornish croft, furze field for fuel).
Cremyll	Crimmell 1249. Cornish crim pol, crooked pool?
Eddystone	Strong currents
Empacombe	Impa (personal name) + coombe, cum, valley. Cornish or Empty Coombe.
Finnygook	Dialect, fynny, bent coarse grass + gook, sunbonnet or sunshade. conical straw covers were used to cover bee hives in winter and the shape could refer to off-shore rocks.
Forder	Old English, forde, ford
Freathy	Dialect, freath, a gap in a hedge OR freathed out, ragged, could refer to rocks
Insworke	Ineswerke, c1250. Old English gweorc, fortification Cornish + ennis, island
Liscawn	Lanscawen 1360. Cornish Lan, nan, valley: scawen, elder tree
Maker	Cornish magor, old or ruined walls
New Invention	(Cove south of Cawsand Beach) Cornish ughel, high + fenten, spring
Pemberknowse	Cornish Pen berth, bush point + nose or point (same meaning as pen)
Port Wrinkle	Porth Wrickel 1605. Cornish, porth, landing place + Wrickle, possible personal name
Pendeen	Cornish Pen, head; dinas, fortress
Penlee	Penleigh, 1359 Pen, head; + Cornish version of Welsh llech flat stones
Penmillard	Cornish Pen, head, mel (moyle), bare; ar, high.
Polhawn	Cornish pol, pool or anchorage + haun, haven, same meaning repeated
Rame	Possibly old English for fortification Pendenhar, the old Cornish name for Rame, Pendeen + hor, ram.

Sconner	Rosconner, 1280 Ros, heath + Cynfor or Conomorus, personal name
Sharrow Cove	Sharapytt 1566. Shara's Pit?
Sheviock	Saviock, Domesday; Sevioc 1226. Old English sevy + oak or Cornish sevi + ek, 'strawberry place'.
Tregantle	Cornish Tre, farm + gantle, Gandle, personal name
Tregonhawke	Cornish Tre + cun, chief or leader + personal name
Venton	Cornish fenten, spring
Wiggle	Cornish gothal, thicket
Withnoe	Cornish, possibly personal name

References: *Place Names of Cornwall*, J. G. Gover. *Cornish Place Names*, O. J. Padel (Alison Hodge 1988).

Portwrinkle Fishermen's Co-operative, about 1880

Celebrations for King Goerge V's Coronation, Cawsand, 1910

Bibliography

Cornwall and its People — A K Hamilton Jenkings (David and Charles reprint paperback. 1970)

A New History of Plymouth — Crispin Gill (David & Charles 1966 & 1979)

Archaeological Survey of the Rame Peninsula — Charles Thomas ICS — 1974

Industrial Archaeology of the Tamar Valley — Frank Booker. (David & Charles 1967)

Industrial Archaeology of Plymouth — Cynthia Gaskell-Brown (1980 — WEA)

Coast Defences of England & Wales — Ian V Hogg

Smuggling Days and Smuggling Ways — Cdr H N Shore. (1892 — National Library 1929)

Cornish Shipwrecks Vol I — Richard Larn and Clive Carter (David & Charles 1969)

Red Rocks of Eddystone — Fred Majdalany (Longmans 1959)

Estuary and River Ferries of S W England — Martin Langley (Waine 1984)

Passenger Steamers of the River Tamar — Alan Kittridge (Twelveheads 1984)

Sea Angling Supreme — Mike Millman (Cassell 1979)

Green Lane Walks in S E Cornwall — Liz Luck (Green Lanes Project. 1985)

Survey of Cornwall — Richard Carew 1602. ed. F E Halliday

The Buildings of Cornwall — N Pevsner. Penguin 1970

The Millbrook May Day Ship — R N Worth. in Report and Transactions of the Devonshire Association Vol XV 1883

Old Cornish Inns — H L Douch (Bradford Barton 1968)

Plymouth's Defences — F W Woodward, (FWW 1990)